SO-AWK-207

SAMS
Teach Yourself
HTML and XHTML

Deidre Hayes

in 10 Minutes
THIRD EDITION

SAMS

201 West 103rd St., Indianapolis, Indiana 46290 USA

Sams Teach Yourself HTML and XHTML in 10 Minutes, Third Edition

ACQUISITIONS EDITOR
Betsy Brown

DEVELOPMENT EDITOR
Heather Goodell

MANAGING EDITOR
Charlotte Clapp

PRODUCTION EDITOR
Katie Robinson

INDEXER
Eric Schroeder

TECHNICAL EDITOR
Rafe Colburn

TEAM COORDINATOR
Amy Patton

INTERIOR DESIGNER
Gary Adair

COVER DESIGNER
Aren Howell

PAGE LAYOUT
Michelle Mitchell

Copyright © 2002 by Sams Publishing

All rights reserved. No part of this book shall be reproduced, stored in a retrieval system, or transmitted by any means, electronic, mechanical, photocopying, recording, or otherwise, without written permission from the publisher. No patent liability is assumed with respect to the use of the information contained herein. Although every precaution has been taken in the preparation of this book, the publisher and author assume no responsibility for errors or omissions. Nor is any liability assumed for damages resulting from the use of the information contained herein.

International Standard Book Number: 0-672-32254-4

Library of Congress Catalog Card Number: 2001090441

Printed in the United States of America

First Printing: September 2001

04   03   02   01   4   3   2   1

Trademarks

All terms mentioned in this book that are known to be trademarks or service marks have been appropriately capitalized. Sams Publishing cannot attest to the accuracy of this information. Use of a term in this book should not be regarded as affecting the validity of any trademark or service mark.

Warning and Disclaimer

Every effort has been made to make this book as complete and as accurate as possible, but no warranty or fitness is implied. The information provided is on an "as is" basis. The author and the publisher shall have neither liability nor responsibility to any person or entity with respect to any loss or damages arising from the information contained in this book.

Contents

About the Author

Deidre Hayes is an information architect with a Web services group that created and manages a very successful corporate intranet. She is continually looking for ways to increase productivity with online workflow technologies and has spoken to national audiences on her favorite Web-related topics: information design and usability. She is a member of the Society for Technical Communications, the Usability Professionals Association, and the HTML Writers' Guild.

Acknowledgments

I would like to thank my family and friends who had to listen to me talk about this book for a long time. Thanks also to the editing staff at Sams Publishing for their help.

Tell Us What You Think!

As the reader of this book, *you* are our most important critic and commentator. We value your opinion and want to know what we're doing right, what we could do better, what areas you'd like to see us publish in, and any other words of wisdom you're willing to pass our way.

You can e-mail or write me directly to let me know what you did or didn't like about this book—as well as what we can do to make our books stronger.

Please note that I cannot help you with technical problems related to the topic of this book, and that due to the high volume of mail I receive, I might not be able to reply to every message.

When you write, please be sure to include this book's title and author as well as your name and phone or fax number. I will carefully review your comments and share them with the author and editors who worked on the book.

Email: webdev@samspublishing.com

Mail: Mark Taber
            Associate Publisher
            Sams Publishing
            201 West 103rd Street
            Indianapolis, IN 46290 USA

Introduction

If you're reading this book, you must have some idea of what HTML and XHTML are, right? Maybe you already know that HTML is the language of the Internet and that far from being a complex programming language requiring years to perfect, HTML is actually a simple markup language that you can learn very quickly. XHTML is the latest version of HTML. You'll learn more about how these two standards work together to create Web pages in later chapters.

You're probably thinking that if you knew how to create documents in HTML, you could help your company earn more money, or better yet, help *you* earn more money.

What you probably don't know is how to get started. How do you learn that language and what's it going to cost?

Getting Started

Guess what? You can create HTML documents on any computer system because HTML works the same on any type of computer. Even better, you can use software that you already own to do it. Any kind of text editor (such as Microsoft Notepad) can be used.

Because we're covering a lot in 10 minutes, it will certainly help as you go through this book if you already have some basic computer skills (including the ability to use a word processor, some understanding of how to use directories and filenames on your computer system, and some experience using a Web browser such as Netscape or Internet Explorer).

What Is the *Sams Teach Yourself in 10 Minutes* Series?

Sams Teach Yourself HTML and XHTML in 10 Minutes uses a series of lessons that walk you through the basics of HTML, and then moves on to more advanced features of the language. Each lesson is designed to take about 10 minutes and each is limited to a particular feature, or several related features, of the HTML language. There are plenty of examples and screen shots to show you what things look like. By the time you finish this book, you should feel confident in creating your own HTML documents for the World Wide Web. You can even use HTML to provide unique and valuable services to your organization, or to tell the world about yourself.

Special Sidebars

In addition to the explanatory text and other helpful tidbits in this book, you will find icons that highlight special kinds of information.

 Plain English sidebars appear whenever a new term is defined. If you aren't familiar with some of the terms and concepts, watch for these flagged paragraphs.

 Caution sidebars alert you to common mistakes and tell you how to avoid them. These paragraphs also explain how to undo certain features, and highlight differences between HTML and XHTML.

 Tip sidebars explain shortcuts (for example, key combinations) for performing certain tasks.

Conventions Used in This Book

The creation and editing of HTML documents can be done using any one of a wide variety of editing tools. You'll find many excerpts from HTML documents that illustrate the points being made. These fragments look like this:

```
<html>
<head><title>This is the Title of Your Page</title></head>
<body>This is the document text surrounded
by HTML tags.</body>
</html>
```

If you're working along with the examples, you might want to enter the HTML fragments into your own HTML documents as you move through the lessons.

Web Browser Screen Shots

Web browsers (such as Internet Explorer and Netscape) are used to interpret HTML documents for your computer. There are many different types of Web browsers (some with more bells and whistles, some with less), but they all do essentially the same thing. You'll find out about some of these differences (and how to avoid problems) as we move through the lessons in this book. To avoid confusion, all the Web browser screen shots in this book were taken from Internet Explorer.

LESSON 1

What's It All About?

In this lesson, you will learn how the Internet works and why HTML and XHTML are so important.

What Is the Internet?

Like many inventions, the Internet began as the solution to a problem. It began with the government's need to find a way to link several computer networks together so that files could be shared. In other words, it created a network of networks. These computer networks were located all over the world and sharing information the old-fashioned way took a long time. Today, the idea of sharing files with people around the world doesn't sound like such a big deal when almost everyone has the modem, e-mail, and dial-up connections that make Wide Area Networks (WANs) commonplace. Back then, however, no one had even considered the idea. So, how did they do it? Well, researchers working for the Advanced Research Projects Agency (ARPA) created ARPAnet, which became the first WAN. Eventually, this led to an *Internet Protocol (IP)*—a common computer language, or protocol—enabling all computers to talk to each other.

Internet Protocol (IP) A predefined set of rules used to enable computers to communicate with each other, regardless of which operating system they are running.

This protocol and the new network of networks made exchanging information much easier than ever before, but it still wasn't simple. To find information on the Internet, you had to know where it was stored. You first had to understand how all the computers were connected, and then you had to navigate through the network to find the data you were looking for.

All that changed in the early 1990s. At that time, a new protocol was created. That protocol, the *Hypertext Transfer Protocol (HTTP)*, enabled information on the Internet to be accessed from *anywhere*, by *anyone*. It's what allows you to jump from one Web page to another by pointing and clicking. The code that makes up the HTTP was a breakthrough, but it can't do everything by itself. The information stored on the computers in the network (the documents and data) must include its own set of communication tools so that the other computers in the network can interpret it. In the case of the World Wide Web, the communication tool is *HTML*.

> **HTML**   Stands for Hypertext Markup Language. Most documents that appear on the World Wide Web were written in HTML.

What Is HTML?

In the Introduction, you learned that HTML is a markup language, not a programming language. In fact, the term HTML is an acronym that stands for Hypertext Markup Language. You can apply this markup language to your pages to display text, images, sound and movie files, and almost any other type of electronic information. You use the language to format documents and link them together, regardless of the type of computer with which the file was originally created.

Why is that important? You know that if you write a document in your favorite word processor and send it to a friend who doesn't have that same word processor, your friend can't read the document, right? The same is true for almost any type of file (including spreadsheets, databases, and bookkeeping software). Rather than using some proprietary programming code that can only be interpreted by a specific software program, HTML is written as plain text that any Web browser or word processing software can read. The software does this by identifying specific elements of a document (such as heading, body, and footer), and then defining the way those elements should behave. These elements, called *tags*, are created by the *World Wide Web Consortium (W3C)*. You'll learn more about tags in upcoming lessons.

Tags These are elements of a Web page that are used to define how those pages should behave. They are most often used in pairs, which surround the element they are defining.

World Wide Web Consortium (W3C) Members of this group develop the protocols that make up the World Wide Web. Currently, the W3C has 180 members from commercial, academic, and governmental organizations worldwide.

Then, What's XHTML?

XHTML, an acronym for eXtensible Hypertext Markup Language, is the first big change to HTML in years. With it, the W3C is trying to add the structure and extensibility of *XML* to HTML pages. By adding a few simple structural elements to existing HTML pages, you can be assured that your Web pages are compatible with later versions of HTML, and even with XML. Lesson 2, "Creating Your First Page," has all the information you need to get started.

XHTML Stands for eXtensible Hypertext Markup Language. It is the latest, and more structured, version of HTML.

XML   Stands for eXtensible Markup Language. It is the newest language being developed by the W3C, and is also the most flexible. You'll learn more about it in Lesson 17, "XML and the Future of the Internet."

How Do They Work?

Markup languages such as HTML and XHTML serve another important purpose when it comes to sharing information over long distances: Information comes to you faster because your computer (using a Web browser) does the work of interpreting the format of the information after you receive the page. Sound confusing? Well, let's look at it another way.

Your computer has a Web browser, such as Internet Explorer or Netscape Navigator, installed on it. When you are looking for information on the Web, your browser has to find the computer that is storing that information. It does this using the HTTP. The storage computer, or server, then sends the new Web page (as a plain text file) back to your computer using the same HTTP. Your browser sees the new Web page and interprets the text and HTML tags to show you the formatting, graphics, and text that appear on the page.

 Tip   HTTP isn't the only protocol used on the Internet. Each protocol is used for a specific network service, such as electronic mail or file transfers. Web browsers use HTTP to read files from other protocols.

Getting Connected

This might be apparent, but sometimes it pays to state the obvious: Although you can create Web page files in any plain text editor and view them in any browser, you have to decide how you are going to store the files. You already know that you can't surf the Net without having an *Internet Service Provider (ISP)*. In the same way, you need a *Web*

Presence Provider (WPP)—or your own Web server—to store your pages before they can be viewed from the Web. Other ways to view Web pages also exist. Table 1.1 describes the methods you can use to store your files.

TABLE 1.1   Storing and Viewing Your Documents

If you store your files on	They can be viewed by people with access to
Your own computer	Your computer (or an *intranet*)
A disk or CD-ROM	That disk or CD-ROM
A Web host server	The World Wide Web

> **Internet Service Provider (ISP)**   A company that provides you with access to the Internet.

> **Intranet**   This is like your own private Internet in that it uses the same HTTP as the World Wide Web, but it is accessible only by people within your own network.

> **Web Host**   A company that stores (hosts) information that can be accessed from the Internet using the HTTP. A Web host may also be called a *Web Presence Provider (WPP)*.

In this lesson, you've learned:

- HTML and XHTML are markup languages that define the structure, rather than the format, of the text elements in your documents.

- HTML is platform independent. As long as they have a browser, your Web site visitors can see the same Web page on a PC, a Macintosh, or a UNIX computer.

- XHTML, the latest version of HTML, requires more structure than HTML.

- You need a Web server or a Web Presence Provider to store your pages before they can be viewed from the Web.

LESSON 2
Creating Your First Page

In this lesson, you will learn to create, save, and view simple Web pages.

Getting Started

I think you'll find that the best way to learn is to follow along with the examples in this book and create your own Web pages as you read. As you learned in the introduction of this book, you can create Web pages or HTML documents with any text editor (including Microsoft Notepad, DOS edit, Mac SimpleText, and UNIX vi). You probably already have at least one of these editors installed on your computer, even if you have never used it before.

 Caution Although you can also create Web pages using some word processors (such as Microsoft Word) and some *WYSIWYG* programs (such as Microsoft FrontPage), I suggest that you ignore these programs for now and concentrate on learning HTML. HTML authoring tools are discussed in Lesson 15, "Web Page Authoring Tools."

WYSIWYG An acronym for What You See Is What You Get. It generally refers to software programs that enable you to see what the page looks like without seeing all the program's formatting codes.

HTML Required Elements

To see what HTML looks like and learn the most basic HTML tags, let's look at a very simple HTML document. Figure 2.1 shows a simple Web page in Microsoft Notepad. You can type the same text in your own editor to follow along with the lesson.

FIGURE 2.1   The <html> and </html> tags are all you need to identify your file as an HTML file.

Every HTML document must begin with the <html> tag and end with its complement, the </html> tag. In addition to the <html> tag, this document includes three other pairs of tags that should be included in any HTML document.

- The <head> and </head> tags are used to indicate any information about the document itself. You'll learn how to add some of this information in later lessons.

- The <title> and </title> tags are used to add a title to your browser's Title bar. The Title bar is the colored band at the top of any application that gives the name of the application.

- The <body> and </body> tags are used to surround any text that appears in the HTML page.

All HTML documents are separated into two parts: the head and the body. Because the title is information about the document, the <title> and </title> tags are placed within the <head> and </head> tags.

Tip   Most HTML tags come in pairs. You use the first tag in the pair (for example, <html>) to tell the computer to start applying the format. The second tag (for example, </html>) requires a slash in front of the tag name that tells the computer to stop applying the format. The first tag is usually referred to by the name within the bracket (for example, HTML). You can refer to the second tag as the end, or the close, tag (for example, end HTML).

One More Page

If you were to create another simple HTML page, you would see that the same four tags are present in this document as well. Only the text that appears between tags is changed.

```
<html>
<head>
<title>My Second Web Page</title>
</head>
<body>
<p>This is my second Web page.</p>
</body>
</html>
```

Saving and Viewing an HTML Page

To view your own page in a browser, you must first save it. Because you've created an HTML document, you want to save your file with an .htm extension (first.htm, for example) so that you recognize it quickly.

Caution   Some people like to name their HTML files with an .html extension (for example, first.html). Some older computer systems, however, still require the file extension to be three characters or fewer and might have trouble reading (or storing) a file with a longer extension.

You can preview any HTML file in your browser, even when that file is stored on your computer rather than on a Web server. In Internet Explorer, you can view your new file by selecting Open from the File menu. Figure 2.2 shows how Internet Explorer displays the first.htm file that you created in Figure 2.1.

 Tip   Although you don't see them, HTML commands are sitting behind the scenes of every document that you open in your Web browser. You can see the HTML commands by selecting Source from the View menu of Internet Explorer (other browsers might use different menu commands). When you find a page on the Web that you like, you can view the source code to learn how you can use HTML to create something similar.

FIGURE 2.2   My First Web Page as it appears in the Internet Explorer browser. Notice that the Title bar contains the text between the <title> and </title> tags and the body of the browser contains the text between the <body> and </body> tags.

Caution Some Web pages use frames to display more than one HTML page at the same time. (See Lesson 10, "Creating Frames.") To view the source code for this type of page, make sure that you use your mouse to highlight some portion of the page you're interested in before selecting Source from the View menu.

How Browsers Work

As great as Web browsers are, you should be aware of some limitations. Although all HTML commands are the same, not all browsers interpret the commands in the same way. Some browsers, such as Lynx, can only display text (even if the HTML author added images to the document). Some older browsers do not understand the newer HTML commands and might produce errors rather than text. What's more, some of the newest browsers enable viewers to determine which window display sizes, fonts, and colors they prefer when viewing Web pages (even if those settings are different from what you, the Web author, want them to see).

Don't despair; there is good news. Most Web pages look the same, or almost the same, on every browser regardless of the computer system: PC, Macintosh, or UNIX. With each lesson in this book, you'll find tips to help ensure that your pages are viewed as you intended. Keep these tips in mind as you create your own Web pages, and you'll avoid the disappointment that many novice Web authors face as they realize that the page they worked so hard on looks awful on another computer or browser.

 Tip The Web itself offers Web page designers the opportunity to preview their pages on a number of different browsers at one time. Web sites, such as the Web Site Garage (www.websitegarage.com), show you exactly how each browser will interpret your page. You can use this information to redesign your page and help ensure that most people see it the way you intend.

XHTML Required Elements

XHTML, the latest revision of HTML, adds another required element to your Web pages: the `<!DOCTYPE>` tag. This tag appears at the top of the file and identifies the file as an HTML document conforming to the XHTML requirements. If you were to create an XHTML-conforming document, it would look like the following:

```
<!DOCTYPE html
    PUBLIC "-//W3C//DTD XHTML 1.0 Transitional//EN"
    "DTD/xhtml1-transitional.dtd">
<html xmlns="http://www.w3.org/1999/xhtml"
    xml:lang="en" lang="en">
<head>
<title>My XHTML Page</title>
</head>
<body>
<p>This is my first XHTML page.</p>
</body>
</html>
```

The `<!DOCTYPE>` tag has three variations: strict, transitional, or frameset. You declare which one you are using in the top of the file.

- **Strict**   Declare this variation when you are certain that your viewers will be accessing your pages from newer browsers that interpret style sheets correctly. You'll learn more about style sheets in Lesson 5, "Adding Your Own Style." The strict variation looks like this:

```
<!DOCTYPE html
    PUBLIC "-//W3C//DTD XHTML 1.0 Strict//EN"
    "DTD/xhtml1-strict.dtd">
```

- **Transitional**   Declare this variation when you are not certain how your viewers will be accessing your pages. This book uses the transitional variation in most instances.

```
<!DOCTYPE html
    PUBLIC "-//W3C//DTD XHTML 1.0 Transitional//EN"
    "DTD/xhtml1-transitional.dtd">
```

- **Frameset**   Declare this variation when you are working in frames. You will learn more about frames in Lesson 10.

```
<!DOCTYPE html
    PUBLIC "-//W3C//DTD XHTML 1.0 Frameset//EN"
    "DTD/xhtml1-frameset.dtd">
```

 Caution   The `<!DOCTYPE>` tag is the only tag that appears in uppercase. All other HTML tags should be lowercase.

You might have noticed one more change from the HTML required elements: The `<html>` tag has some new attributes: `xmlns`, `xml:lang`, and `lang`. In HTML, you only have to include the `<html>` tag to identify the document as an HTML file, but XHTML requires that you use the `xmlns` attribute to link your document to the W3C's definition of XHTML, which doesn't exist yet. It's a bit confusing, but it is all an attempt to plan for the future. You will learn more about these plans and how to prepare in Lesson 17, "XML and the Future of the Internet." For now, just remember to include the `<!DOCTYPE>` tag and the full `<html>` tag (shown in the following HTML sample) in all your Web pages. Figure 2.3 demonstrates how the XHTML page, created previously, would appear in the browser.

```
<!DOCTYPE html
    PUBLIC "-//W3C//DTD XHTML 1.0 Transitional//EN"
    "DTD/xhtml1-transitional.dtd">
<html xmlns="http://www.w3.org/1999/xhtml"
    xml:lang="en" lang="en">
```

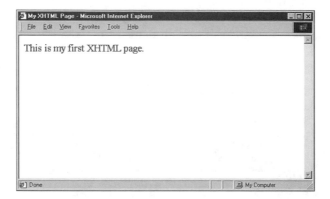

Figure 2.3   Notice that adding the XHTML declaration does not affect your page's appearance.

Don't Forget the Basics

Tags aren't the only things that make a good Web page. As you continue through the lessons in this book, you'll discover that while HTML was very forgiving, XHTML must conform to the rules. Though current versions of the most popular browsers will recognize your intentions even if you use incorrect tags (or enter the correct tags in the wrong order), later versions will not. You'll want to move beyond the novice level now and follow some basic Web coding principles to conform to XHTML's standards. Following is a brief list of those principles, but you'll learn more in later lessons:

- *Include all the required XHTML elements that you learned in this lesson*   You might want to create a template for yourself that already includes these tags. You can use the XHTML document created in the "XHTML Required Elements" section as a template. Whenever you create a new Web page; open your template file, add your new text, and save the new file.

- *Use lowercase for all tags*   To the browser, <HEAD>, <Head>, and <head> all mean the same thing. (That won't always be true.) Use the same lowercase spelling for all your commands and you won't be caught having to recode your pages as the standard evolves.

- *Never use spaces in filenames*   Older computer systems have trouble reading filenames that include spaces (for example, *my first page.htm*). Instead, you can use a couple of file management tricks to replace the spaces.

  1. Use an underscore (_) to represent spaces (for example, my_first_page.htm).

  2. Use initial capital letters to indicate new words in a filename (for example, MyFirstPage.htm).

Table 2.1 shows a list of the tags that you learned in this lesson. A similar table of new HTML tags appears at the end of other lessons.

Table 2.1   HTML Tags Used in This Lesson

HTML Tag	Closing	Description of Use
<!DOCTYPE>		Begins each XHTML document and includes a reference to the strict, transitional, or frameset variation.
<html>	</html>	Surrounds all the text in an HTML file. Must include the xmlns, xml:lang, and lang attributes.
<head>	</head>	Contains information about the document.
<title>	</title>	Identifies the title of the page and is used within the <head> tag.
<body>	</body>	Surrounds the text of the page.

In this lesson, you've learned:

- Any text editor, including Microsoft Notepad, can be used to create Web pages (or HTML documents).

- All HTML documents are separated into two parts: the head and the body.

- Every HTML document must include the `<html>` tag and end with its complement, the `</html>` tag.

- Every XHTML document must include the correct variation of the `<!DOCTYPE>` tag before the `<html>` tag.

- All HTML tags (except the `<!DOCTYPE>` tag) should be typed in lowercase.

LESSON 3
Adding Text and More

In this lesson, you will learn how to use HTML to add text and headings in your Web pages. You'll also learn how to add mathematical notations, information about your Web page, and special characters (such as ampersands).

Paragraphs

You might not realize it, but you already learned how to create an HTML paragraph in Lesson 2, "Creating Your First Page." In HTML, a paragraph is created whenever you insert text between the <p> tags. Look at the code from Lesson 2 again:

```
<!DOCTYPE html
     PUBLIC "-//W3C//DTD XHTML 1.0 Transitional//EN"
     "DTD/xhtml1-transitional.dtd">
<html xmlns="http://www.w3.org/1999/xhtml"
      xml:lang="en" lang="en">
<head>
<title>My First Web Page</title>
</head>
<body>
<p>This is my first Web page.</p>
</body>
</html>
```

Web browsers see that you want text and they display it. Web browsers don't pay any attention to how many blank lines you put in your text; they only pay attention to the HTML tags. In the following HTML code, you see several lines of text and even a blank line, but the browser only recognizes paragraphs surrounded by the <p> and </p> tags (or paragraph tags). The <p> tag tells the browser to add a blank line before displaying any text that follows it, as shown in Figure 3.1.

```
<!DOCTYPE html
      PUBLIC "-//W3C//DTD XHTML 1.0 Transitional//EN"
      "DTD/xhtml1-transitional.dtd">
<html xmlns="http://www.w3.org/1999/xhtml"
      xml:lang="en" lang="en">

<head>
<title>Typing Paragraphs in HTML</title>
</head>
<body>
<p>This is the first line.

But is this the second?</p>
<p>No, this is.</p>
</body>
</html>
```

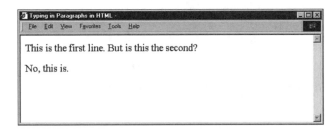

FIGURE 3.1 The browser ignores the blank line that I inserted and puts the line break before the <p> tag instead.

Web browsers do something else with paragraph text that you should be aware of: They wrap the text at the end of the browser window. In other words, when the text in your Web page reaches the edge of the browser window, it automatically continues on the next line regardless of where the <p> is located.

The <p> tag always adds a blank line, but you might not always want a blank line between lines of text. Sometimes you just want your text to appear on the next line (such as the lines of an address or a poem). You can use a new tag for this—the line break, or <br /> tag, shown in Figure 3.2.

This new tag forces the browser to move any text following the tag to the next line of the browser, without adding a blank line in between. Figure 3.3 shows how the browser uses these two tags to format your text.

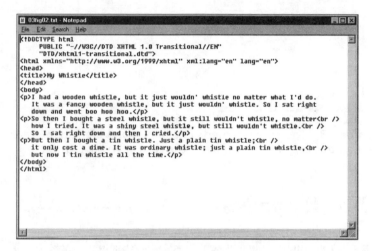

FIGURE **3.2**   The <p> and <br /> tags help to separate your text into lines and paragraphs.

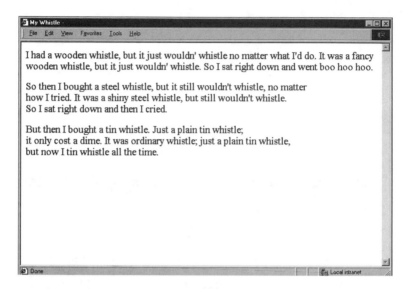

FIGURE 3.3 The browser inserts line breaks and blank paragraph separators only where you place the correct HTML tags.

Text Emphasis

So far you've learned how to add text, but here you will learn how to format it. You will occasionally want to add emphasis to your text to make it stand out. HTML enables you to quickly apply some standard formats, such as boldface and italic, using a predefined set of tags. All these tags occur in pairs (corresponding opening and closing tags) and must surround the text that they are emphasizing. Use the HTML code that follows in your own Web page to see how each of these tags appears in the browser.

```
<!DOCTYPE html
    PUBLIC "-//W3C//DTD XHTML 1.0 Transitional//EN"
    "DTD/xhtml1-transitional.dtd">
<html xmlns="http://www.w3.org/1999/xhtml"
    xml:lang="en" lang="en">
<head>
<title>Emphasizing Text</title>
</head>
```

```
<body>
<p>Make your text one size larger with the
   <big>big tag.</big></p>
<p>Try the <b>bold tag</b> or the <strong>strong tag</strong>
   to make an impact.</p>
<p>The <i>italics tag</i> and the <em>emphasis tag</em>
 create a different impact.</p>
<p>Use the <tt>teletype tag</tt> to imitate a typewriter.</p>
<p>Make your text one size smaller with the
   <small>small tag.</small></p>
</body>
</html>
```

 Caution   Other formatting tags exist in HTML, but their use is discouraged in HTML and deprecated in XHTML in favor of style sheets. The World Wide Web Consortium (W3C) has determined that HTML should be used to identify types of information (text, headings, tables, and so on), but should not be used to format that information.

Deprecated   Some older HTML tags, specifically related to formatting, have been replaced by the formatting capabilities of style sheets.

Style Sheets   Web developers use style sheets to specify formatting instructions for a single document or a group of documents.

You'll learn how to create style sheets in Lesson 5, "Adding Your Own Style." Throughout the book, however, you'll see how styles can enhance your Web pages.

Headings

Separating your text into paragraphs isn't the only way to format your Web pages. HTML enables you to add six different heading tags to your pages by using the tags <h1>–<h6>. These tags are very simple to use. Look at the following line of code:

```
<h1>This is Heading 1</h1>
```

The closing heading tags also create an automatic paragraph break. In other words, all headings automatically include a blank line to separate them from the text. Heading 1, the <h1> tag, has the largest font of the heading tags and Heading 6, the <h6> tag, has the smallest. In fact, you usually only see Web page authors use the <h1>–<h3> tags because the remaining tags, <h4>–<h6>, are actually smaller than normal text. Figure 3.4 shows a sample of all the heading tags compared to normal text.

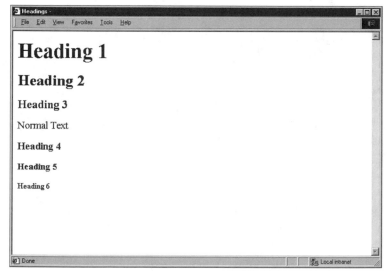

FIGURE 3.4   Notice that HTML's Heading 4 is the same size as normal text, but Headings 5 and 6 are actually smaller.

Tip   Unless you or the people viewing your pages have adjusted the browser's default settings, normal HTML body text appears in 12 point Times New Roman font on most computer systems.

Special Characters

You might find that you sometimes need to use symbols on your Web pages. Symbols (such as +, –, %, and &) are used frequently in our everyday writing, so it's easy to understand that they would appear on a Web page as well. Unfortunately, not all Web browsers display these symbols correctly. HTML uses a little computer shorthand, either using a numerical code or a text code (called an entity character reference) to tell the browser how to interpret these symbols. Table 3.1 shows some of the most frequently used codes.

Table 3.1   Special Character Codes

Char	Code	Description
&	&amp;	ampersand
<	&lt;	less than
>	&gt;	greater than
©	&copy;	copyright
®	&reg;	registered trademark
±	&plusmin;	plus or minus
^{2}	&sup2;	superscript 2
^{3}	&sup3;	superscript 3
´	&acute;	acute accent

Table 3.1 Continued

Char	Code	Description
`	`	grave accent
#	#	number
%	%	percent

The W3C's Web site (www.w3.org/TR/REC-html40/sgml/ _entities.html#h-24.2.1) contains a complete list of the characters supported by HTML. You can see how many of these symbols are easy to understand (for example, & for the ampersand and > for the greater than symbol). Some of the characters, such as number and percent, require that you memorize numbered codes. Yuck. The best thing you can do is to make sure that you preview your Web pages in a variety of browsers before publishing them.

 Tip Here's a special character that you should remember: . The symbol' stands for *nonbreaking space* and is used to insert a space inside an HTML document. Because HTML ignores extra spaces between words and tags, you need to have a way of including an extra space. You can do that with the   character.

Math and Science Notations

Although HTML was first designed and used by scientists, it has yet to support mathematical and scientific notation with any degree of complexity. HTML does give you two tags to help write simple equations. Together with the codes for special characters, the <sub> (subscript) and <sup> (superscript) tags go a long way toward creating equations, as shown in Table 3.2.

Table 3.2   `<sup>` and `<sub>` Tags

You Type	The Browser Displays
A² + B² = C²	$A^2 + B^2 = C^2$
CO₂ = Carbon Dioxide	CO_2 = Carbon Dioxide

If you are looking to write more complex equations, you need to be a little more creative. The obvious answer is to write your equation in the program that you usually use, and then use a graphics program to turn it into an image. You can insert that image into any HTML page, as you've already learned. That works, but the solution is limited. Because the equation is graphical, you are not able to index or search for text within the equation. That's a big drawback, but so is the fact that images slow down your page's load time and the fact that your equation cannot be viewed by nongraphical Web browsers.

 Tip   Some commercial products are available to help you notate mathematical expressions. You can see a list of them on the W3C Web site (www.w3.org/Math/).

English Isn't the Only Language

You can use HTML even if you don't write in English. URLs, hyperlinks, HTML tags, and document formatting elements are language neutral, but text requires a specification all its own. If you write in standard U.S. English, you don't need to make any changes to the way you create your HTML documents. If you are writing text in any other language, however, you should specify the language for the browser. The following HTML samples show the designations for British, English, and French.

```
<html xmlns="http://www.w3.org/1999/xhtml"
      xml:lang="en-br" lang="en-br">
```

and

```
<html xmlns="http://www.w3.org/1999/xhtml"
      xml:lang="fr" lang="fr">
```

The language attributes (xml:lang and lang) support the same values as ISO, the International Standards Organization. You can see the full list of supported languages and their codes at www.oasis-open.org/cover/iso639-2a.html.

Tip   Why is language important? Browsers do not recognize the language you type unless you use the lang attribute. Some search engines use the lang attribute to return only pages written in a specific language. Speech synthesizers use this information to aid in pronunciation. Even some spelling checkers can use the information to recognize misspellings.

Mixing Languages in a Single Page

Although the preceding example shows the lang attribute used as part of the <html> tag at the top of your document, it's possible that you would want to include text of one language within a document of another language—for example, including a paragraph in French within a document in English. You can assign the lang attribute to the <p> tag to solve this problem. Look at the following sample:

```
<!DOCTYPE html
     PUBLIC "-//W3C//DTD XHTML 1.0 Transitional//EN"
     "DTD/xhtml1-transitional.dtd">
<html xmlns="http://www.w3.org/1999/xhtml"
     xml:lang="en-US" lang="en-US">
<head>
<title>Multi-Language Document</title>
```

```
</head>
<body>
<p>put your English text here.</p>
<p lang="fr">mettez votre texte français ici.</p>
<p lang="en-US">put the rest of your English text here.</p>
</body>
</html>
```

Meta Tags

Finally, you get to do something with the <head> tag. So far, you've only seen the <title> tag used to give information about the document, but you can do a lot more with the <head> tag. What's more, aside from the <title> tag, meta information doesn't usually appear in your document. You can use the meta information tag (<meta>) to identify the page's author, keywords used for searching, or a brief description to appear in search results. You also can use the <meta> tag to give commands to the browser. You can use as many <meta> tags as you like in your page. You'll learn how in the sections that follow.

Improved Searching

Search engines (as you'll find in Lesson 17, "XML and the Future of the Internet") add the content of your Web pages to their indexes. When a potential visitor enters a search phrase, the search engine checks its index to find that word and returns any pages that include that word. It works great. But, what if you were a realtor and you worked hard at creating a Web page that included the words houses, housing, sale, and buy; but didn't include the phrase real estate? If that was the phrase your visitor was looking for, they would never find your page.

You can use the <meta> tag to include product names, geographic locations, industry terms, and synonyms that people might be searching for. There are three <meta> tags that work to help improve your chances of being found by a search engine:

- *Keywords*—Keywords are words that you feel people might use to search for your Web page, or synonyms for words in your document.

- *Description*—This is usually a paragraph of information about your page. Some search engines use it to describe your page, but other search engines use the first few lines of text in your document.

- *Author*—This is your opportunity to shine. Just in case someone is searching for your name, they will find it if you enter that information into the <meta> tag.

Meta information for search engines comes in pairs: name and contents. The following HTML code includes meta information pairs for each of the preceding <meta> tags. Remember, the <meta> tags always appear between the <head> tags.

```
<!DOCTYPE html
     PUBLIC "-//W3C//DTD XHTML 1.0 Transitional//EN"
     "DTD/xhtml1-transitional.dtd">
<html xmlns="http://www.w3.org/1999/xhtml"
     xml:lang="en" lang="en">
<head>
<title>Your HTML Page</title>
<meta name="keywords" contents="words that people might
                        use to search for your page." />
<meta name="description" contents="a brief paragraph
                        describing your document." />
<meta name="author" contents="your name" />
</head>
<body>
<p>insert your document here.</p>
</body>
</html>
```

Refresh and Redirect

There might be times when you want to replace one page with another or want to redirect a link. You might, for example, choose to include a *splash page* on your Web site. You can use the meta information to force the page to change within a given time span using the sample code that follows:

```
<meta http-equiv="refresh" content="time in seconds,
                                    new URL" />
```

> **Splash Page** The introductory page used by some Web page authors to show flashy graphics or a product logo before continuing to the rest of the site's contents.

If you have a page that you update several times a day and you want to make sure that people always see the most recent version, you can enter the page's own URL in the refresh tag. When the browser sees the refresh tag, it presents the requested URL in the specified time.

```
<meta http-equiv="refresh" content="time in seconds,
                                    URL for this page" />
```

> **Caution** Because not all Web browsers support this attribute, authors should include some content on the splash page that enables users to move to the next page on their own.

Expiration Dates

If you have a page that you change frequently, you can specify an expiration date in the <meta> tag to ensure that the Web browser looks for a newer version (rather than displaying an older version, which might still be stored in the browser's memory). Look at the example that follows:

```
<meta http-equiv="expires"
      contents="Wed, 04 July 2001 00:00:00 GMT" />
```

When you enter the URL for this page in your browser, it checks its history files to see whether a copy is stored there. If so, it checks the meta information to see whether this page is still valid. If the expiration date has passed, the browser looks to the Web for a more recent copy before displaying the page.

Table 3.3 reminds you of the formatting tags you learned in this lesson.

Table 3.3   HTML Tags Used in This Lesson

HTML Tag	Closing	Description of Use
`<b>`	`</b>`	Text appears boldface.
`<big>`	`</big>`	Text appears one size larger than normal.
` `		Line break. Forces text to the next line.
`<em>`	`</em>`	Text appears emphasized (italic). Usually the same as `<i>`.
`<h1>`	`</h1>`	A first-level heading.
`<h2>`	`</h2>`	A second-level heading.
`<h3>`	`</h3>`	A third-level heading.
`<h4>`	`</h4>`	A fourth-level heading. Rarely used.
`<h5>`	`</h5>`	A fifth-level heading. Rarely used.
`<h6>`	`</h6>`	A sixth-level heading. Rarely used.
`<i>`	`</i>`	Text appears emphasized (italic).
`<meta />`		Identifies information about the document.
`<p>`	`</p>`	Paragraph break. Forces a blank line.
`<small>`	`</small>`	Text appears one size smaller than normal.

Table 3.3 Continued

HTML Tag	Closing	Description of Use
`<strong>`	`</strong>`	Text appears boldface. Same as `<b>`.
`<sub>`	`</sub>`	Text appears in subscript.
`<sup>`	`</sup>`	Text appears in superscript.
`<tt>`	`</tt>`	Text appears monospaced, as if typed.

In this lesson, you've learned:

- The `<p>` tag, or paragraph tag, tells the browser to add a blank line before it displays any text that follows. The `<br />` tag moves your text to the next line without adding a blank line.

- HTML enables you to add emphasis to your text with several predefined formatting tags.

- Symbols such as +, −, and % require a little computer shorthand to tell the browser how to interpret these symbols. This shorthand begins with an ampersand (&) and ends with a semicolon (;).

- You can add other languages to your HTML documents by using the `lang` attribute on the `<html>` tag.

- Meta information for search engines comes in pairs: `name` and `contents`, and the `<meta />` tags always appear between the `<head>` tags.

LESSON 4
Linking Text and Documents

In this lesson, you will learn how to use HTML's most valuable feature: hyperlinks.

What Is a URL?

Ask anyone and they'll tell you that (far and away) the feature that makes HTML so worthwhile is the capability to *hyperlink* from one place to another. All Web pages, Internet resources, files, and so on, have an address. That address is known as a *Uniform Resource Locator*, or URL. Before you can link to another page (or resource), you have to know its address. You can find the URL for any resource in the Address box (or Location box) of your browser.

> **Hyperlink** The text that enables you to jump from a Web document to another location.

> **Caution** Although URL is the commonly accepted term to describe the location of Internet resources, a new term URI (Uniform Resource Identifier) will likely replace it as XML becomes the standard. You'll find out more about XML in Lesson 17, "XML and the Future of the Internet."

The <a> tag (called an anchor) is used to define hyperlinks. Unlike most other HTML tags, the <a> tag *requires* an attribute. When you use the <a> tag, you must specify whether you want the enclosed text to link *to* some- place (with the <a href="*the URL you want to link to*"> tag) or be linked *from* someplace (with the <a name="*the place in a document you want to link to*" id="*the place in a document you want to link to*"> tag). The following section provides some examples.

Hyperlinks

The easiest link to learn is the hyperlink to another location. The <a> tag with the href attribute and its closing tag, </a>, surround any text that you want to highlight. The default hyperlink highlighting in HTML is underlined blue text. In the following example, you would click on the words click here to jump (hyperlink) to the document found at the URL inside the quotes.

```
Please <a href="http://www.microsoft.com">click here</a> to
open the Microsoft Web site.
```

Tip   Did you know that you can copy the URL of any Web page from your browser? Just highlight the address in the Address box (or Location box) and select Edit, Copy (or press Ctrl+C). Then, select Edit, Paste (or press Ctrl+V) to paste the address between the quotes of the href attribute.

Linking to Other Files and E-mail

You can link to more than just other people's Web sites. You can use the same href attribute to link to e-mail addresses for other pages of your own Web site, or even to other files on your own computer. The hyperlink to point to another file (second.htm) on *my* own computer, for example, is shown in the following code. In this example, the second.htm file is stored in the same directory as the page linking to it.

```
Please <a href="second.htm">click here</a> to open
    my second Web page.
```

If, however, my second.htm file was stored in another directory (for example, the Links directory), the hyperlink would need to include the directory name too, as in the following:

```
Please <a href="links/second.htm">click here</a> to open
    my other page.
```

 Tip   Did you know that you can force your hyperlink to open a new browser window? This is especially handy if you want to link to someone else's Web site without directing traffic away from your own site. Use the `target="_blank"` attribute, as in the following example. Try it!

```
<a href="http://www.somewhere.com/page.htm"
    target="_blank">
    Click here</a> to open a related Web site.
```

The `href` attribute changes slightly if you want to link to a file that is not part of your Web site. You need to tell the Web browser that the file is not located on the Web server. You can see how that is accomplished in the following example:

```
<a href="file:\\servername\foldername\filename.extension">
    Click here</a> to open my favorite file.
```

If I want to link to my dogs.doc file in the 4legs folder of my animals server, for example, my hyperlink looks like the following:

```
<a href="file:\\animals\4legs\dogs.doc">click here</a>
    to open my favorite file.
```

Caution Did you notice that the direction of my slashes changes when I change my link type from `http://` to `file:\\`? The forward slash (/) is always used to separate directory folders on a Web file server. The backslash (\) is used to separate directory folders in Windows and DOS.

You also can link to an e-mail address by using the `mailto` prefix, as shown in the following code line. When you click on the words `click here`, an e-mail window that enables you to type your message to Mickey Mouse appears.

```
<a href="mailto:mickey.mouse@disney.com">Click here</a>
   to send mail to Mickey.
```

Linking Within the Same Page

Now that you know how to link to other resources, you might want your hyperlinks to be more meaningful. HTML enables you to use hyperlinks to point to a specific spot (or anchor) in an HTML document, instead of just pointing to the entire document. As an example, suppose you have a list of headlines at the top of your HTML document that points to a more complete article at the bottom of your document. This is easy in HTML. Remember that anchor tags come with three attributes: `href` (which has already been discussed), and `name` and `id` (which always appear together).

Anchor A named point on a Web page. The same tag is used to create hyperlinks and anchors.

 Caution In the new XHTML and XML standards (which will eventually replace HTML), the W3C is calling for the use of a new attribute for the `<a>` tag (called id) to replace the name attribute. The smart thing to do (to make sure that you comply with the new standard when it is released) is to use both attributes in your documents.

The <a> tag also enables you to name an anchor (or bookmark) in your document with the name and id attributes. HTML then enables you to use the anchor tag to point directly to that bookmark. Figure 4.1 demonstrates how the example in the previous paragraph might look in HTML. Figure 4.2 shows that same document in the browser.

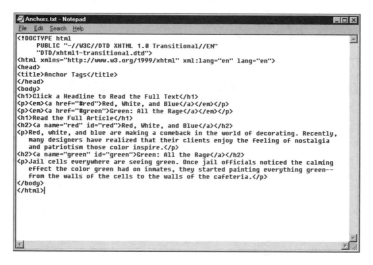

```
Anchors.txt - Notepad
File  Edit  Search  Help
<!DOCTYPE html
     PUBLIC "-//W3C//DTD XHTML 1.0 Transitional//EN"
     "DTD/xhtml1-transitional.dtd">
<html xmlns="http://www.w3.org/1999/xhtml" xml:lang="en" lang="en">
<head>
<title>Anchor Tags</title>
</head>
<body>
<h1>Click a Headline to Read the Full Text</h1>
<p><em><a href="#red">Red, White, and Blue</a></em></p>
<p><em><a href="#green">Green: All the Rage</a></em></p>
<h1>Read the Full Article</h1>
<h2><a name="red" id="red">Red, White, and Blue</a></h2>
<p>Red, white, and blue are making a comeback in the world of decorating. Recently,
    many designers have realized that their clients enjoy the feeling of nostalgia
    and patriotism those color inspire.</p>
<h2><a name="green" id="green">Green: All the Rage</a></h2>
<p>Jail cells everywhere are seeing green. Once jail officials noticed the calming
    effect the color green had on inmates, they started painting everything green--
    from the walls of the cells to the walls of the cafeteria.</p>
</body>
</html>
```

FIGURE 4.1   Notice how the href attribute points to the location named by the name and id attributes.

 Caution   The <a href> tag includes the same URL format you've seen before, but also includes the # symbol to separate the filename from the named anchor.

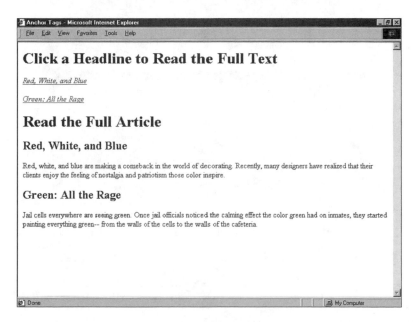

FIGURE **4.2**   The <a> tag with the href attribute is highlighted, but the <a> tag with the name and id attributes is not.

Tip   When naming anchors, remember to keep the names short and not to use spaces. These aren't HTML requirements, but following these guidelines certainly makes linking easier. Look at the example in Figure 4.1 again. The named anchor for the Red, White, and Blue article is the abbreviated red.

Linking to an Anchor in Another Page

Creating a hyperlink to an anchor in another page requires only one more element: the URL. As you learned before, you can link to an anchor in a file on your own Web site, as shown in Figure 4.3, or you can link to a known anchor in a file on another Web site. The keyword in that sentence is *known*. You can't link to a specific spot on a file unless that spot is already recognized by the Web browser as a named anchor.

```
Headlines.txt - Notepad                                    _ □ ×
File  Edit  Search  Help
<!DOCTYPE html
      PUBLIC "-//W3C//DTD XHTML 1.0 Transitional//EN"
      "DTD/xhtml1-transitional.dtd">
<html xmlns="http://www.w3.org/1999/xhtml" xml:lang="en" lang="en">
<head>
<title>Anchor Tags</title>
</head>
<body>
<h1>Click a Headline to Read the Full Text</h1>
<p><em><a href="articles/colors.htm#red">Red, White, and Blue</a></em></p>
<p><em><a href="articles/colors.htm#green">Green: All the Rage</a></em></p>
</body>
</html>
```

FIGURE 4.3 Notice that each href attribute includes a folder name (articles), a filename (colors.htm), and the specific anchor name (red).

 Tip You can use style sheets to add visual interest to your hyperlinks. Lesson 5, "Adding Your Own Style," will show you how.

Table 4.1 lists the HTML tags that were discussed in this lesson.

TABLE 4.1 HTML Tags Used in This Lesson

HTML Tag	Closing	Description of Use
<a href="...">	</a>	Surrounds text that links to another location.
<a name="...">	</a>	Surrounds text that is linked to.
<a id="...">	</a>	Same as <a name>, but might soon replace it. Use them together as: <a name="..." id="...">.

In this lesson, you've learned:

- Anchor tags come with three attributes: href (which links *to* someplace), and name and id (which link *from* someplace).

- You can copy the URL of any Web page from your browser and paste it between the quotes of the href attribute in your <a> tag.

- The same href attribute links to e-mail addresses, to other pages of your own Web site, or even to other files on your own computer.

LESSON 5
Adding Your Own Style

In this lesson, you will learn how to create style sheets, apply them to your HTML pages, and wow your audience with your creativity.

Style Sheets

As you've already learned, HTML was written as a markup language for defining the structure of a document (paragraphs, headings, tables, and so on). Although it was never intended to become a desktop publishing tool, it does include some basic formatting attributes, such as bgcolor, font-size, and align. In 1996, the W3C first recommended the idea of Cascading Style Sheets (CSS) to format HTML documents. The recommendation, which was updated in mid-1998, enables Web developers to separate the structure and format of their documents.

> **Style Sheet** A set of rules that determine how the styles are applied to the HTML tags in your documents.

The CSS recommendation describes the following three types of style sheets: embedded, inline, and linked.

- **Embedded** The style properties are included (within the <style> tags) at the top of the HTML document. A style assigned to a particular tag applies to all those tags in this type of document. In this book, you'll see embedded style sheets most often.

- **Inline**   The style properties are included throughout the HTML page. Each HTML tag receives its own style attributes as they occur in the page.

- **Linked**   The style properties are stored in a separate file. That file can be linked to any HTML document using a `<link>` tag placed within the `<head>` tags.

In the following sections, you'll learn how to construct these style sheets and how to apply them to your documents.

 Tip   Even without all the formatting benefits that style sheets provide, Web developers can rejoice in knowing that using style sheets will no doubt be the biggest timesaver they've ever encountered. Because you can apply style sheets to as many HTML documents as you like, making changes takes a matter of minutes rather than days.

Before style sheets, if you wanted to change the appearance of a particular tag in your Web site; you would have to open each document, find the tag you wanted to change, make the change, save the document, and continue on to the next document. With style sheets, you can change the tag in a single style sheet document and have the changes take effect immediately in all the pages linked to it.

Defining the Rules

Style sheet rules are made up of selectors (the HTML tags that receive the style) and declarations (the style sheet properties and their values). In the following example, the selector is the `body` tag and the declaration is made up of the style property (`background`) and its value (`black`). This example sets the background color for the entire document to black.

```
body {background:black}
```

You can see that, in a style sheet, the HTML tag is not surrounded by brackets as it would be in the HTML document, and the declaration is surrounded by curly braces. Declarations can contain more than one property. The following example also sets the text color for this page to white. Notice that the two properties are separated by a semicolon.

```
body {background:black; color:white}
```

You can format this style rule in a number of ways to make it easier to read. For example, the following rule produces exactly the same results as the preceding style:

```
body {background:black;
     color:white}
```

So does this:

```
body {
     background:black;
     color:white
     }
```

If you want to apply the same rules to several HTML tags, you could group those rules together, as in the following example:

```
body, td, h1 {
               background:black;
               color:white
               }
```

Add a Little `class`

As the old saying goes, rules are made to be broken. What if you don't want every single h1 heading in your document to be white on a black background? Maybe you want every other h1 heading to be yellow on a white background. Let me introduce you to the `class` attribute. You can apply this attribute to almost every HTML tag, and it's almost like creating your own tags.

Figure 5.1 shows a fairly standard HTML page that uses an aqua table at the top of the page to hold the navigation links, and places other tabular content in yellow tables throughout the document. You can see the HTML document for that page in Figure 5.2.

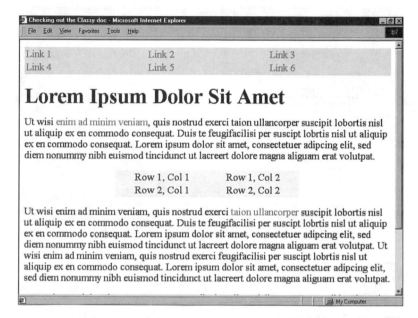

FIGURE 5.1   An HTML page that formats two tables differently.

Take a closer look at the style properties in Figure 5.2. This document defines two `table` styles within the `<style>` tags. The HTML tag name `table` is followed by a period (`.`) and the `class` names (`nav` and `rest`).

```
table.nav {background:aqua}
table.rest {background:yellow;
            text-align:center;
            color:black}
```

When the table is referenced in the body of the document, you must apply the `class` attribute to tell the browser which style properties should be applied. The HTML markup for each table in this example appears in the following HTML code. You can see that the `class` name appears within quotations just like the other HTML attributes (and as with the `width` attribute shown here).

```
<table class="nav" width="100%">
<table class="rest" width=50%>
```

```
classy_doc.html - Notepad                                           _ 8 X
File  Edit  Search  Help
<!DOCTYPE html
      PUBLIC "-//W3C//DTD XHTML 1.0 Transitional//EN"
      "DTD/xhtml1-transitional.dtd">
<html xmlns="http://www.w3.org/1999/xhtml"
      xml:lang="en" lang="en">
<head>
<title>Checking out the Classy doc</title>
<style type="text/css">
table.nav {background:aqua}
table.rest {background:yellow;
           text-align:center;
           color:black}
a:link {color:red;
        text-decoration:none}
</style>
</head>
<body>
<table class="nav" width="100%">
<tr><td><a href="here.htm">Link 1</a></td><td><a href="here.htm">Link 2</a></td><td><a href="here.htm
<tr><td><a href="here.htm">Link 4</a></td><td><a href="here.htm">Link 5</a></td><td><a href="here.htm
</table>
<h1>Lorem Ipsum Dolor Sit Amet</h1>
<p>Ut wisi <a href="here.htm">enim ad minim veniam</a>, quis nostrud exerci taion ullancorper sus
feugiFacilisi per suscipt lobrtis nisl ut aliquip ex en commodo consequat. Lorem ipsum dolor sit
nonnumy nibh euismod tincidunct ut lacreert dolore magna aliguam erat volutpat.</p>
<div align="center">
<table class="rest" align="center" width="50%">
<tr><td>Row 1, Col 1</td><td>Row 1, Col 2</td></tr>
<tr><td>Row 2, Col 1</td><td>Row 2, Col 2</td></tr>
</table>
</div>
<p>Ut wisi enim ad minim veniam, quis nostrud exerci <a href="here.htm">taion ullancorper</a> sus
feugiFacilisi per suscipt lobrtis nisl ut aliquip ex en commodo consequat. Lorem ipsum dolor sit
nonnumy nibh euismod tincidunct ut lacreert dolore magna aliguam erat volutpat. Ut wisi enim ad m
lobrtis nisl ut aliquip ex en commodo consequat. Lorem ipsum dolor sit amet, consectetuer adipcim
nonnumy nibh euismod tincidunct ut lacreert dolore magna aliguam erat volutpat.</p>
```

FIGURE 5.2   The HTML document for the page in Figure 5.1.
Notice the class attribute in each <table> tag.

Applying Styles

Before moving on, we'll quickly cover how to apply style properties to
your documents. Remember, you have three methods to add style sheets:
embedded, linked, and inline. We'll discuss each one in turn.

 Tip   In designing your Web site, use linked style
sheets to describe your most frequently used styles
(the ones that will be formatted in the same fashion
for all of the pages in your Web site), such as the
heading tags and link tags. Use embedded style sheets

to describe the formatting of tags that will remain the same within a single document, or set of documents, such as special table settings or page margins. Use the inline style sheets to describe the formatting of tags that vary from the site-wide formatting applied with the other style sheets, such as for a special callout or sidebar.

Embedded Styles

All the styles are defined at the top of the HTML document within the <head> tags because they contain information about the entire document. The styles defined here apply only to the one document in which they appear. If you plan to use these same styles in another document, you need to add them there as well.

```
<head>
<style type="text/css">
table.nav {background:aqua}
table.rest {background:yellow;
            text-align:center;
            color:black}
a:link {color:red;
        text-decoration:none}
</style>
</head>
```

Tip The <style> tag almost always includes the type="text/css" attribute, so you should get used to adding it.

Linked Styles

Linked style sheets hold all the style properties in a separate file. You then link the file into each HTML document where you want those style properties to appear.

```
<head>
<link rel="stylesheet" href="mystyles.css" type="text/css">
</head>
```

With this method, I've created a separate file called mystyles.css (for cascading style sheet) that contains all my style properties. You can see that the same `type="text/css"` attribute shows up here. Following are the entire contents of the mystyles.css file. These are the same styles that showed up in the preceding embedded styles example, but now they appear in a separate text file.

```
table.nav {background:aqua}
table.rest {background:yellow;
            text-align:center;
            color:black}
a:link {color:red;
        text-decoration:none}
```

 Tip Well-designed Web sites (with more than one page) contain repeated page elements and styles. The linked style sheet is most appropriate for this type of Web authoring. You'll learn more about designing effective Web sites in Lesson 13, "Designing with HTML."

Inline Styles

With inline styles, the style properties are added to the HTML tag as the tag is entered. This means that if I want the same style to appear on all the `<h1>` tags in my document, I would have to type those styles in all the `<h1>` tags. Look at the following example. I am still using the same style properties, as in the previous examples, but now you can see how the two tables would be created using inline styles.

```
<table style="background:aqua" width="100%">

<table style="background:yellow; text-align:center;
              color:black" width="100%">
```

Using inline styles, the `<style>` tag becomes the `style` attribute. Multiple style properties are still separated by semicolons, but the entire group of properties for each tag is grouped within each HTML tag. This type of style sheet is fine for documents in which you only need to apply styles to one or two elements, but you wouldn't want to do all that work when you have a lot of styles to add.

Cascading Precedence

You've got one more thing to learn before moving on. These three styles are not treated equally by the browsers, nor are they supposed to be.

Web browsers give precedence to the style that appears closest to the tag. So, inline styles (which appear as attributes within the tag itself) are most important. Embedded styles (which appear at the top of the HTML file) are applied next, and linked styles (which appear in another file altogether) are applied last.

Imagine that you have created an embedded style for the `<h1>` tag, but want to change that style for one occurrence of the `<h1>` tag in that document. You would create an inline style for that new `<h1>` tag. The browsers recognize that fact and change the style for that tag to reflect the inline style.

 Caution Style sheet precedence is supposed to place more importance on embedded styles than on linked style sheets. In actual practice, however, you'll find that both Internet Explorer and Netscape treat linked sheets as more important than embedded sheets (but they do treat inline styles as more important than either of the other two). You'll find that you have better luck if you use either linked or embedded styles, but not both.

Formatting Text with Styles

Text is the most important element of any Web page. Without text, there is nothing on the page to help people decide whether it's worth coming back.

Text on an HTML page is structured by the <body>, <p>, <td>, <tr>, <th>, <h1>–<h6>, and <li> tags (among others). You can add your own style preferences to each of these tags using the style properties shown in Table 5.1.

 Tip Unless you (or the people viewing your pages) have adjusted the browser's default settings, normal HTML body text appears in 12 point Times New Roman font on most computer systems.

In the following example, we've added some embedded style elements that set the font, font size, and font color for the body text of the basic HTML document we created in Lesson 2, "Creating Your First Page." In Figure 5.3, you can see how those styles change the appearance of the document in the browser.

```
<!DOCTYPE html
     PUBLIC "-//W3C//DTD XHTML 1.0 Transitional//EN"
     "DTD/xhtml1-transitional.dtd">
<html xmlns="http://www.w3.org/1999/xhtml"
     xml:lang="en" lang="en">
<head>
<title>My First Web Page</title>
<style type="text/css">
body {font-family:"Arial";
     font-size:"12pt";
     color:red}
</style>
</head>
<body>
<p>This is my <b><i>first</i></b> Web page.</p>
</body>
</html>
```

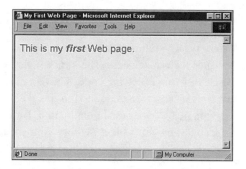

FIGURE 5.3   The browser applies the style attributes to the text in the <body> tags.

Table 5.1   Style Properties for Text

Property	Description of Use and Values
background	Sets the background color for the text.
color	Sets the text color for the text.
font-family	Sets the font for the text.
font-size	Can be a point size, a percentage of the size of another tag, or xx-small to xx-large.
font-style	normal (which is assumed)or italic.
font-weight	extra-light to extra-bold.
text-align	left, right, center, or justify (full).
text-indent	Can be a fixed length or a percentage.
text-decoration	underline, overline, strikethrough, and none.

Microsoft maintains a brief tutorial for style sheets on their typography
site (`http://www.microsoft.com/typography/web/default.`
`htm?fname=%20&fsize=`). The tutorial teaches Web page authors how
style sheets can enhance their documents. The `<style>` tag for one of
those examples is shown in the following code. This is impressive because
of the many different styles and classes defined in this document. You can
see that you are only limited by your own imagination. Be sure to see this
style sheet and others on Microsoft's older Gallery Web site at
`http://www.microsoft.com/typography/css/gallery/slide3.htm`.

```
<style type="text/css">
body {background: coral}
.copy {color: Black;
    font-size: 11px;
    line-height: 14px;
    font-family: Verdana, Arial, Helvetica, sans-serif}
a:link {text-decoration: none;
    font-size: 20px;
    color: black;
    font-family: Impact, Arial Black, Arial,
                Helvetica, sans-serif}
.star {color: white;
    font-size: 350px;
    font-family: Arial, Arial, helvetica, sans-serif}
.subhead {color: black;
    font-size: 28px;
    margin-top: 12px;
    margin-left: 20px;
    line-height: 32px;
    font-family: Impact, Arial Black, Arial,
                Helvetica, sans-serif}
.what {color: black;
    font-size: 22px;
    margin-left: 20px;
    font-weight: bold;
    font-style: italic;
    font-family: Times New Roman, times, serif}
.quott {color: black;
    font-size: 120px;
    line-height: 120px;
    margin-top: -24px;
    margin-left: -4px;
    font-family: Arial Black, Arial, helvetica, sans-serif}
.quotb {color: black;
```

```
           font-size: 120px;
           line-height: 120px;
           margin-right: -1px;
           margin-top: -33px;
           font-family: Arial Black, Arial, helvetica, sans-serif}
.quote {color: red;
        font-size: 24px;
        line-height: 28px;
        margin-top: -153px;
        font-family: Impact, Arial Black, Arial,
                     Helvetica, sans-serif}
.footer {color: cornsilk;
         background: red;
         font-size: 22px;
         margin-left: 20px;
         margin-top: 16px;
         font-family: Impact, Arial Black, Arial,
                      Helvetica, sans-serif}
.headline {color: black;
           font-size: 80px;
           line-height: 90px;
           margin-left: 20px;
           font-family: Impact, Arial Black, Arial,
                        Helvetica, sans-serif}
.mast {color: cornsilk;
       font-size: 90px;
       font-style: italic;
       font-family: Impact, Arial Black, Arial,
                    Helvetica, sans-serif}
</style>
```

 Caution None of the most popular Web browsers react the same way to all the style sheet properties. Your best bet is to remember to test everything before you publish it. Web Review maintains a table of style sheet properties mapped to the most popular browsers. Check out this table (http://www. webreview.com/style/css1/charts/mastergrid.shtml) to find out whether the style sheet properties you plan to use are supported by specific browsers.

Link Styles

You have probably seen those bright blue underlined hyperlinks on the Web. Style sheets have the following selectors to help you change the look of them:

- `a:link`   Sets the styles for unvisited links.

- `a:visited`   Sets the styles for visited links.

- `a:active`   Sets the styles for the link while it is linking.

- `a:hover`   Sets the style for the link while your mouse is hovering.

Table 5.2 shows some of the style properties you can assign to your links.

Table 5.2   Style Properties for the Anchor Styles

Property	Description of Use and Values
`background-color`	Sets the background color for the link.
`color`	Sets the text color for the link.
`font-family`	Sets the font for the text of the link.
`text-decoration`	`underline`, `overline`, `strikethrough`, and `none`.

 Tip   One of the most popular style sheet effects on the Web right now is to remove the underlining on hyperlinks. To do this on your pages, just add the `text-decoration:none` declaration to the `a` styles, as shown in the following example:

```
a:link {color:yellow;
        text-decoration:none}
```

If you like the look of the underlined hyperlink, you're in luck. You don't have to specify anything at all. Underlining is assumed for all `a` styles.

Color Styles

As you can see in Table 5.3, you can apply color to your HTML tags in two different ways: with `color` or with `background`.

 Tip Check out `http://wdvl.internet.com/Graphics/Colour/` for a quick tune-up of Web color selections.

Table 5.3   Style Properties for Color

Property	Description of Use and Values
color	Sets the color of the text.
background	Sets the background of the page or text.

 Caution Don't forget to test your pages before you publish them. Not all colors work together. If you've specified a black background color and a black text color, you've got a problem because no one will be able to see your text.

Adding Lines

A horizontal line, or horizontal rule as it is named in HTML, is one of the easiest tags to use. You can insert the `<hr />` tag anywhere in your document to insert a horizontal line that extends across the space available. Take a look at the following sample HTML. It shows three `<hr>` tags: two used as a section break between text and the other used inside a table cell. Figure 5.4 shows how they appear in the browser.

```
<!DOCTYPE html
    PUBLIC "-//W3C//DTD XHTML 1.0 Transitional//EN"
    "DTD/xhtml1-transitional.dtd">
<html xmlns="http://www.w3.org/1999/xhtml"
```

```
        xml:lang="en" lang="en">
<head>
<title>Horizontal Lines</title>
<style type="text/css">
td {text-align=center}
</style>
</head>
<body>
<p>This is a horizontal line.</p>
<hr />
<p>This is another horizontal line.</p>
<hr />

<table width="50%" rules=cols>
  <tr>
    <td>This is also a<hr />horizontal line.</td>
    <td>There is <br />no line on this<br />side
        of the table.</td>
  </tr>
</table>
</body>
</html>
```

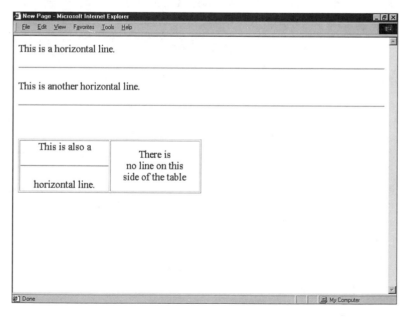

FIGURE 5.4 The <hr /> tag inserts a horizontal line that stretches across the available horizontal space.

Adding Style to Horizontal Lines

As with other HTML tags, you can use style sheet properties to design your own horizontal rules. You can set the height, width, and color of the line to match the design of your Web page. The following HTML sample shows two different styles attached to the <hr /> tag. If I use the hr.red style, I see a red line that takes up 50 percent of the horizontal space. If I use the hr.purple style, I see a purple line that is 4 pixels high and takes up 75 percent of the horizontal space.

```
<style type="text/css">
hr.red {color:red;
        width:50%}
hr.purple {color:purple;
           height:4;
           width:75%}
</style>
```

I've used both of those styles in the following sample HTML. Figure 5.5 shows you how those examples look in the browser.

```
<!DOCTYPE html
     PUBLIC "-//W3C//DTD XHTML 1.0 Transitional//EN"
     "DTD/xhtml1-transitional.dtd">
<html xmlns="http://www.w3.org/1999/xhtml"
     xml:lang="en" lang="en">
<head>
<title>Horizontal Lines</title>
<style type="text/css">
td {text-align=center}
hr.red {color:red;
        width:50%}
hr.purple {color:purple;
           height:4;
           width:75%}
</style>
</head>
<body>
<p>This is a plain horizontal line.</p>
<hr />

<p>This is a purple horizontal line.</p>
<hr class="purple" />

<table width="50%" rules=cols>
```

```
<tr>
  <td>This is a red <hr class="red" />horizontal line.</td>
  <td>There is <br />no line on this<br />
      side of the table.</td>
</tr>
</table>
</body>
</html>
```

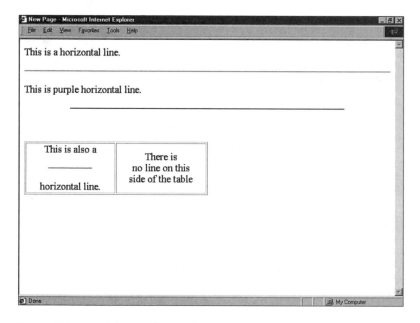

FIGURE 5.5   Applying styles to the `<hr />` tag changes the appearance of the horizontal line.

Margin Styles

Style sheets give you another important advantage: You can specify the margins of almost any HTML element. The margins can be defined in pt, in, cm, or px sizes.

```
body {margin-left: 100px;
      margin-right: 100px;
      margin-top: 50px}
```

You can set the `margin-left`, `margin-right`, and `margin-top` properties individually or combine them into one property called `margin` that applies the sizes to the `top`, `right`, and `left` margins.

```
body {margin: 100px 100px 50px}
```

The sample CSS document from Microsoft's CSS Gallery (which you looked at earlier) also specifies margins for the text elements. Try it on your documents.

```
<style type="text/css">
body {background: coral }
.subhead { color: black;
    font-size: 28px;
    margin-top: 12px;
    margin-left: 20px;
    line-height: 32px;
    font-family: Impact, Arial Black, Arial,
                 Helvetica, sans-serif}
</style>
```

Tip   Check out the following style sheet references for more help:

- `http://webdeveloper.com/html/html_css_1.html` Web Developer's CSS tutorial

- `http://webreview.com/pub/Style_Sheets` Web Review's CSS references

- `www.w3.org/TR/REC-CSS2/propidx.html` W3C's list of CSS properties

- `http://www.microsoft.com/typography/web/default.htm?fname=%20&fsize=` Microsoft's CSS tutorial

Table 5.4 lists the HTML tags that were discussed in this lesson.

Table 5.4   HTML Tags Used in This Lesson

HTML Tag	Closing	Description of Use
`<hr />`		Creates a horizontal line
`<style>`	`</style>`	Surrounds style sheet properties, or references to external style sheets. The standard open tag should be `<style type=_"text/css">`.

In this lesson, you've learned:

- The CSS recommendation describes three types of style sheets: embedded, inline, and linked.

- Three different style sheets exist in HTML: embedded, inline, and linked.

- If multiple style sheets are applied to your HTML document, the browser applies the styles of the inline style sheet first, then the linked style sheets, and then embedded style sheets.

- The `<hr />` tag adds a horizontal line to your HTML document. Use style sheet properties to adjust the color, width, and height.

- Remove the underlining on your hyperlinks by adding the `text-decoration:none` declaration to your a styles tags.

LESSON 6
Creating Lists

In this lesson, you will learn to use HTML to organize your text into lists.

Types of Lists

One way to organize the text in your Web pages is with lists. In addition to the obvious benefit of being able to *list* items on a page, they also provide a design benefit by enabling you to break up long pages of ordinary paragraphs. HTML recognizes the following list types and has tags that correspond to each.

 Bulleted (unordered) lists

 Numbered/lettered (ordered) lists

 Definition lists

Tip You should use ordered lists when the items in the list must be followed in a specific order, and use unordered lists when they do not. You generally use definition lists for terms and their definitions, but they can have other uses as well.

Bulleted (Unordered) Lists

A bullet (usually a solid circle) appears in front of each item in an unordered list. HTML automatically creates the bullet when you use the unordered list tag (`<ul>`) together with the list item tag (`<li>`). Although the following sample HTML shows each list item as a single line of text, your list items can be as long as you want.

```
<ul><li>first item in the list</li>
<li>second item in the list</li>
<li>third item in the list</li></ul>
```

Figure 6.1 shows how the Web browser displays an ordered and an unordered list. The figure includes list examples from many of the following sections.

When your list items are longer than a single line of text, the Web browser indents the second line (and any following lines) so that the text lines up.

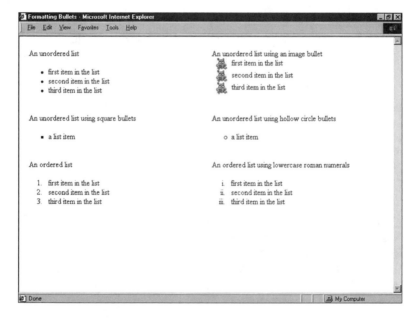

FIGURE 6.1   Ordered and unordered lists shown in the Web browser.

Formatting Bulleted Lists

HTML automatically adds a solid circle in front of each list item as a bullet, but you have two other choices. Using style sheet tags (which you learned about in Lesson 5, "Adding Your Own Style"), you can select one of two other bullet types: a square or a hollow circle. You can see how your HTML document would look if you chose to use a square bullet instead of the standard solid circle. Figure 6.1 shows how the Web browser displays this bullet type.

```
<!DOCTYPE html
    PUBLIC "-//W3C//DTD XHTML 1.0 Transitional//EN"
    "DTD/xhtml1-transitional.dtd">
<html xmlns="http://www.w3.org/1999/xhtml"
    xml:lang="en" lang="en">

<head>
<title>Bulleted Lists</title>
<style type="text/css">
ul square {list-style-type:square}
ul owl {list-style-image:url(owl.jpg)}
</style>
</head>
<body>
<ul class="square">
<li>a list item</li>
<li>another list item</li>
</ul>

<ul class="owl">
<li>a list item</li>
<li>another list item</li>
</ul>
</body>
</html>
```

You'll notice that this sample HTML also includes a style (list-style-image). This style enables you to replace the plain HTML bullets with your own image. In this example, I replaced the bullets with an image of an owl. Add the URL for one of your own images to see how this works on your browser. You can see the owl image in Figure 6.1.

Numbered (Ordered) Lists

If the items in your list should follow a specific order, as in recipes or instructions, you want to use the ordered list tag (<ol>). With this tag, HTML automatically numbers or letters your items for you. Here's an example:

```
<ol><li>first item in the list</li>
<li>second item in the list</li>
<li>third item in the list</li></ol>
```

Notice how similar the two list samples are. Both the <ul> and <ol> tags call for the individual list items to be identified with the <li> tag. Like the <ul> tag, HTML has an automatic style for the list items within the <ol> tag. HTML automatically numbers the items with the familiar arabic numerals (1, 2, 3, and so on). What's more, it automatically renumbers the list items if you decide to add or delete items later. Once again, Figure 6.1 has an example of this type of list.

Formatting Numbered Lists

You can use style sheets for formatting ordered lists. In addition to the standard arabic numerals, there are four other styles that can be applied to your ordered list. Table 6.1 describes each of those types, and the following sample HTML shows how you can use style sheets to create a list ordered by lowercase roman numerals. Figure 6.1 shows an example of such a list in the Web browser.

```
<!DOCTYPE html
     PUBLIC "-//W3C//DTD XHTML 1.0 Transitional//EN"
     "DTD/xhtml1-transitional.dtd">
<html xmlns="http://www.w3.org/1999/xhtml"
     xml:lang="en" lang="en">
<head>
<title>Bulleted Lists</title>
<style type="text/css">
ol.lwroman {list-style-type:lower-roman}
</style>
</head>
<body>
<ol class="lwroman">
<li>a list item</li>
<li>another list item</li>
</ol>
</body>
</html>
```

Table 6.1   List Style Types

Sample	Style Syntax	Definition
a, b, c	lower-alpha	Lowercase letters
A, B, C	upper-alpha	Uppercase letters
i, ii, iii	lower-roman	Small roman numerals
I, II, III	upper-roman	Large roman numerals

Setting a Start Value

There might be times when you'd like to start an ordered list with a number other than one. Many times when writing instructions, you need to interrupt a numbered list with some other material (such as text or examples), and then continue with the numbered list. To do this in HTML, close the first list, add the additional materials that you need, and then start a new list, using the list item's `value` attribute to set the beginning number for the new list. Figure 6.2 demonstrates how the following code is interpreted by the browser.

```
<!DOCTYPE html
    PUBLIC "-//W3C//DTD XHTML 1.0 Transitional//EN"
    "DTD/xhtml1-transitional.dtd">
<html xmlns="http://www.w3.org/1999/xhtml"
    xml:lang="en" lang="en">
<head>
<title>Continuing a List</title>
<style type="text/css">
</style>
</head>
<body>
<p>It's Payday!</p>
<ol>
<li>Turn in your timecard.</li>
<li>Receive your paycheck.</li>
<li>Endorse your paycheck.</li>
</ol>
<p>Congratulations! You're almost there.</p>
<ol>
<li value="4">Put the check in the bank.</li>
```

```
</ol>
</body>
</html>
```

 Caution The value attribute requires that you use Arabic numbering to specify the start value, even if you've chosen roman numerals or letters for your list type.

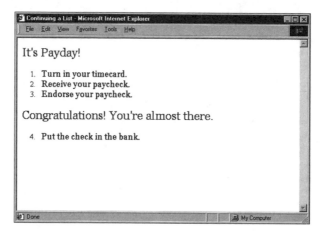

FIGURE 6.2 The Web browser shows an ordered list that was interrupted and started again using the value attribute.

Definition Lists

If you need it, HTML has one more type of list available to you: the definition list, which uses the <dl> tag. Rather than using the usual <li> tag to specify the items in the list, this type of list uses the <dt> tag (for definition terms) and the <dd> tag for their definitions. Following is an example of the HTML for a definition list, and Figure 6.3 shows how the Web browser formats a definition list.

```
<dl><dt>The Definition Term</dt>
<dd>Is defined below the term.</dd></dl>
```

Fɪɢᴜʀᴇ **6.3**   A definition list displayed in the browser.

Table 6.2 lists the HTML tags that were discussed in this lesson.

Table 6.2   HTML Tags Used in This Lesson

HTML Tag	Closing	Description of Use
`<dl>`	`</dl>`	Definition list.
`<li>`	`</li>`	List item. Used with `<ol>` and `<ul>` tags.
`<dt>`	`</dt>`	Definition term. The list item of a `<dl>`.
`<dd>`	`</dd>`	Definition data. Describes definition terms.
`<ol>`	`</ol>`	Ordered, or numbered/lettered, list.
`<ul>`	`</ul>`	Unordered, or bulleted, list.

In this lesson, you've learned:

- HTML recognizes three different list types: bulleted (unordered), numbered (ordered), and definition.

- Rather than the default bullet style (a solid circle), style sheets enable you to select three other bullet types: a square, a hollow circle, or an image of your own.

- The `value` attribute of the `<ol>` tag sets the beginning number for your list.

LESSON 7
Creating Tables

In this lesson, you will learn how to build tables using HTML, and how to control the layout and appearance of a Web page using tables.

Simple Tables

Traditionally, *tables* have been used for displaying tabular data (such as numbers) in rows and columns. The flexibility of HTML, however, enables Web developers to create tables that display more than just numbers. In fact, as important as the capability to display tabular data is, even more important to Web designers is the capability to control the layout of other document elements (such as text and images).

> **Table**   An arrangement of horizontal rows and vertical columns. The intersection of a row and a column is called a *cell*.

 Caution   Although HTML tables look similar to your favorite spreadsheet, HTML tables don't perform mathematical functions.

HTML tables are not difficult to create, but they do require some organization. All HTML tables begin with the `<table>` tag and end with the `</table>` tag. In between those tags are three other tags to be aware of, as follows:

<tr> defines a horizontal row.

<td> defines a data cell within that row.

<th> specifies a data cell as a table heading. In newer browsers, a table heading cell is formatted as centered and bold.

Remember that Web browsers ignore any spaces, tabs, and blank lines that you include in your HTML document. So, feel free to use spacing to help you keep track of the table tags. Figure 7.1 shows enough blank spaces between the tags so that you can see the rows and columns lining up. It makes it easier to ensure that you don't forget any tags. Figure 7.2 shows how that table looks in a browser.

FIGURE 7.1   A simple two column, three row HTML table.

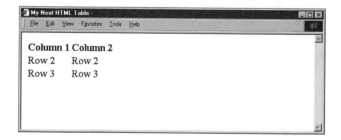

FIGURE 7.2   That same HTML table as it appears in the browser.

Formatting Tables

Now you can add some pizzazz to your simple table. In Table 7.1, you see some of the different style attributes you can apply to HTML tables. Figure 7.3 shows how you can use these attributes to create an HTML table with a little more character. Figure 7.4 shows the way the table appears in a browser.

 Tip The World Wide Web Consortium's Web site (www.w3.org/TR/REC-html40/struct/tables.html) has detailed descriptions of all the attributes available for tables, as well as examples of how you can use them.

Table 7.1 Table Style Attributes

Attribute	Default	Use with	Values
align	left	all	Horizontal alignment of cell contents: left, right, center, and char (which aligns around a specific character, usually a decimal or comma).
bgcolor		all	Background color.
border	0	\<table>	Width of the border (in *pixels*).
cellpadding	0	\<td>, \<th>	Space between border and content (in pixels).
cellspacing	0	\<td>, \<th>	Space between cells (in pixels).

Table 7.1 Continued

Attribute	Default	Use with	Values
colspan	1	`<td>`, `<th>`	Number of columns that a cell should span (merge).
rowspan	1	`<td>`, `<th>`	Number of rows that a cell should span (merge).
rules	none	`<table>`	Where the lines (rules) appear between cells: `rows`, `cols`, or `all`.
valign	center	`<td>`, `<tr>`, `<th>`	Vertical alignment of cell contents: `top`, `bottom`, or `baseline`.
width	to fit	all	Width of table or cells (in pixels or as a percentage of the page).

Pixel A pixel is the size of a single dot of color on your monitor. The monitor's display resolution affects the size of a pixel. A display resolution of 800×600 means that your monitor displays 800 pixels in width by 600 pixels in height. The pixel size on a monitor that displays at a resolution of 1024×800 would be much smaller than one on a monitor with a resolution of 800×600.

A table with a `width` attribute fixed at 800 pixels fills a screen that is set to a resolution of 800×600, but only fills a portion of a screen that is set to 1024×800.

```
next-style.txt - Notepad
File  Edit  Search  Help
<!DOCTYPE html
     PUBLIC "-//W3C//DTD XHTML 1.0 Transitional//EN"
     "DTD/xhtml1-transitional.dtd">
<html xmlns="http://www.w3.org/1999/xhtml" xml:lang="en" lang="en">
<head>
<title>My Next HTML Table</title>
<style type="text/css">
th {color:"red";
    font-family:"Arial"}
td {color:"blue";
    font-family:"Tahoma"}
</style>
</head>
<body>
<table width="50%" borders="1" rules="all">
<tr><th>Column 1</th><th>Column 2</th></tr>
<tr><td align="center">   Row 2</td><td align="center">   Row 2</td></tr>
<tr><td align="center">   Row 3</td><td align="center">   Row 3</td></tr>
</table>
</body>
</html>
```

FIGURE 7.3   Table attributes in HTML.

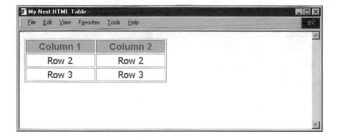

FIGURE 7.4   That same HTML table as it appears in the browser.

Advanced Tables

HTML contains two more attributes that you should be aware of when formatting tables. The `colspan` (which causes a cell to span two or more columns) and `rowspan` (which causes a cell to span two or more rows) attributes are invaluable when creating complex tables, although, as you can tell from the HTML in Figure 7.5, using them makes it harder to keep your HTML document organized. Figure 7.6 shows how the table looks in a browser.

```
next-rules.txt - Notepad                                        _ □ ×
File  Edit  Search  Help
<!DOCTYPE html
     PUBLIC "-//W3C//DTD XHTML 1.0 Transitional//EN"
     "DTD/xhtml1-transitional.dtd">
<html xmlns="http://www.w3.org/1999/xhtml" xml:lang="en" lang="en">
<head>
<title>My Next HTML Table</title>
<style type="text/css">
th {color:"red";
    font-family:"Arial"}
td {color:"blue";
    font-family:"Tahoma"}
</style>
</head>
<body>
<table width="100%" borders="1" rules="all">
<tr><th colspan="2">Columns 1 and 2 are combined</th></tr>
<tr><td align="center">   Row 2</td><td rowspan="2">Rows 2 and 3 are combined.</td></tr>
<tr><td align="center">   Row 3</td></tr>
</table>
</body>
</html>
```

FIGURE 7.5   Using the `colspan` and `rowspan` attributes to create complex tables.

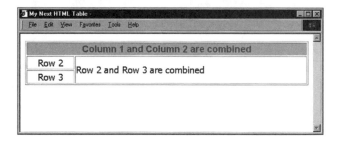

FIGURE 7.6   That same HTML table as it appears in the browser.

Using Tables for Layout

Look at the source code for some of your favorite Web pages and I bet that you'll find they were created using tables. Following are some of my favorite Web pages that contain tables:

www.yahoo.com   The columns of search categories are created with tables.

www.webdeveloper.com   This site is essentially a three column table.

www.microsoft.com   Microsoft, too, uses tables to design the layout of its Web site.

http://disney.go.com/disneyatoz/fan   Disney's Ultimate Fan site shows another creative use of tables in layout.

www.sun.com   Sun's very graphic home page is made up of a series of small images placed in table cells. Breaking up a large image into many smaller images helps the page load faster.

Tip Even if you don't plan to place a border around the cells in your table, it's much easier to see how your HTML commands are interpreted by your Web browser when you have the borders turned on (<table border="1">). After you are satisfied that the table is formatted correctly and your content is where you want it to be, you can remove the border attribute, leaving just the <table> tag.

Table 7.2 lists the HTML tags that were discussed in this lesson.

Table 7.2   HTML Tags Used in This Lesson

HTML Tag	Closing	Description of Use
`<table>`	`</table>`	Identifies the title of the page. Used within the `<head>` tag.
`<td>`	`</td>`	Table data cell. Similar to a column.
`<th>`	`</th>`	Table heading.
`<tr>`	`</tr>`	Table row. Surrounds table cells (`<td>`) and headings (`<th>`).

In this lesson, you've learned:

- Tables control the layout of HTML document elements (such as text, navigation, and images).

- Extra spaces in your HTML documents help you keep track of the table tags. Web browsers ignore any spaces.

- The `colspan` and `rowspan` attributes merge cells in complex tables.

LESSON 8
Adding Images

In this lesson, you'll learn how to add pizzazz to your Web pages with graphic images.

Adding Images

If the Web were nothing but text, it would still be technologically impressive, but it wouldn't be nearly as much fun. Adding images to your pages is easy; adding images that make your Web pages look professional just takes a little know-how. Luckily, you'll learn that here—and it shouldn't take longer than 10 minutes.

The two most frequently used graphics file formats found on the Web are GIF and JPEG. The *Joint Photographic Experts Group (JPEG)*, format is used primarily for realistic, photographic-quality images. The *Graphics Interface Format (GIF)* is used for almost everything else. One new file format is gaining popularity among designers and will soon be making its presence known: the *Portable Network Graphics* format *(PNG)* is expected to replace the GIF format someday. Don't rush out to replace all your graphics, however; not all browsers support it fully yet.

Tip Sound like a pro—learn how to pronounce the graphic formats you use. GIF is pronounced "jif" (like the peanut butter), JPEG is pronounced "jay-peg," and PNG is pronounced "ping."

Let's get down to business. You add all images by using a single HTML tag, the image source tag, `<img src="location" />`. By now you probably recognize that this tag is actually an `<img />` tag with an attribute (`src`) and attribute value (`location`), but because all images require an `src` attribute, it's easier to refer to it as a single tag. You'll also notice that the image tag does not have a corresponding closing tag. It is a single tag and you'll need to remember to add the closing slash at the end: `<img />`. The result of the following sample HTML appears in Figure 8.1.

```
<!DOCTYPE html
     PUBLIC "-//W3C//DTD XHTML 1.0 Transitional//EN"
     "DTD/xhtml1-transitional.dtd">
<html xmlns="http://www.w3.org/1999/xhtml" xml:lang="en"
     lang="en">
<head>
<title> First Images</title>
<style type="text/css">
</style>
</head>
<body>
<p>This is an image in my first Web page.<img
     src="images\happyFace.jpg" /></p>
</body>
</html>
```

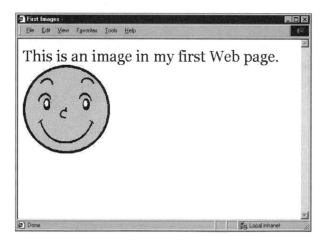

FIGURE 8.1 The `<img src="location" />` tag inserts an image into your HTML document.

Caution Be aware that the World Wide Web Consortium, the standards-setting body for HTML, is considering replacing the `<img />` tag with the more generic `<object>` tag. To add an image using the `<object>` tag, follow this format:

```
<object data="navbar.gif" type="image/gif"> text
       describing the image... </object>
```

Adding Alternate Text

When browsing the Web, you might have noticed that many times when you move your mouse pointer over an image, you see a text pop-up that describes the image, or tells you something more about the area of the Web site that image represents. You can see an example of that type of text pop-up in Figure 8.2.

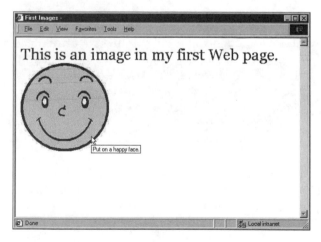

FIGURE 8.2   The `alt` attribute adds a text pop-up to your image.

The following HTML sample shows how the `alt` attribute is added into the `<img />` tag. Like the `src` attribute, the `alt` attribute tells the browser more information about the `image`. And, like the `src` attribute, you should always use the `alt` attribute with the `<img />` tag.

```
<img src="images\happyFace.jpg" alt="Put on a happy face." />
```

> **alt attribute**   Sets the *alternate text* for a graphic. It was named `alt` because it describes the text some people would see as an alternative to the image that others would see.

The `alt` attribute has another very important purpose. Many people with slower modem connections to the Web decide to customize their browser settings to ignore graphics because loading graphics into a Web browser can sometimes take a long time. Remember, too, that not all browsers enable you to view graphics. Some browsers, such as Lynx, have no graphics capabilities at all. The `alt` attribute ensures that people who can't view your graphics can still understand their context.

> **Tip**   Although you should use the `alt` attribute whenever you use the `<img />` tag, make sure that you don't specify irrelevant text. For example, there is no point in specifying an alternate text for a decorative image (such as a bullet or a line); instead, specify an empty value (`alt=" "`).

Without any other attributes, the browser displays the image at its original size and aligns the bottom of the graphic with the bottom of the text. You can adjust both those settings using style sheet tags.

Image Attributes

You can use other attributes of the `<img />` tag to change the image size. Table 8.1 shows some of these attributes, and the following sections provide some examples for adding these attributes to your documents.

Table 8.1   Attributes Used with the <img /> Tag

Attribute	Values	Description of Use
height	pixel or percent	Specifies the height of an image.
width	pixel or percent	Specifies the width of an image.

Adjusting the Height and Width

You can adjust the size of your image using the height and width attributes. You can set these attributes to a fixed pixel size or a percentage of the page size. Look at the following sample HTML lines. The first line sets the happy face image from Figure 8.1 to a fixed pixel size of 100 pixels high and 100 pixels wide. The second line sets the same image to 14 percent of the page width and 27 percent of the page height. Figure 8.3 shows how both of these look in the browser.

```
<img src="images\happyFace.jpg" alt="Put on a happy face."
    height="100" width="100" />
<img src="images\happyFace.jpg" alt="Put on a happy face."
    height="14%" width="27%" />
```

The Web browser interprets pixels and percentages equally well when rendering an image. You need to remember, however, that your Web visitors may not use the same monitor display settings that you do. What does this mean to you? My monitor is set to 800 pixels wide. In the preceding HTML sample, I set the happy face image to 27 percent of the page width, or 216 pixels wide. If I viewed the same page on a monitor set to 1024 pixels wide, that same 27 percent of the page width would now equal 277 pixels, which is much wider than I wanted.

If you truly want the image to be a certain percentage of the page (as you might for a graphical line), then use percentages. Using percentages ensures that the image will take up the space you want it to. If you want the image to appear a specific size, use the pixel setting.

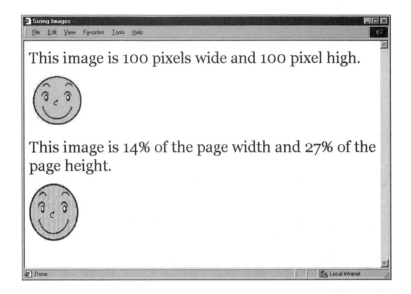

FIGURE **8.3**   The height and width attributes control the size of the image.

 Caution   Be sure to change both the height and width of your image if you plan to resize them. Adjusting only one of them will stretch the image out of proportion. An alternative is to resize the image in your image editor and add the newly sized image without the height and width attributes.

Aligning Text and Images

You can use the align attribute of the <img /> tag to force an image to appear on the left or right of a section of text. You can see an example of this attribute in action in Figure 8.4.

```
<img src="images\happyFace.jpg" alt="Put on a happy face."
    height="60" width="60" align="right" />
```

You also can use the `align` attribute to vertically align an image with the text. The `align` attribute has three more values: `top`, `bottom`, and `center`, which are discussed in the following list. Figure 8.4 shows you a sample HTML document using the vertical alignment properties.

- Setting the `align` attribute to `top` aligns the top of the image with the top of any surrounding text.

- Setting the `align` attribute to `bottom` aligns the bottom of the image with the bottom of any surrounding text.

- Setting the `align` attribute to `center` aligns the center of the image with the center of any surrounding text.

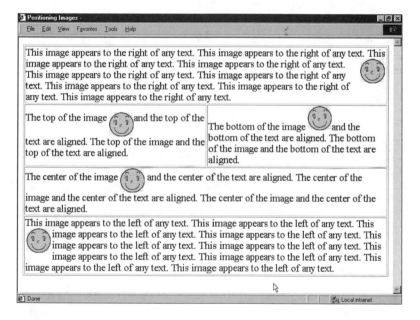

FIGURE 8.4   Notice how the `align` attribute forces the image to align with the text.

Caution Be sure to preview your HTML documents in the browser (or in several browsers) to make sure you are happy with how they look before you publish them. Not all browsers treat these `align` attributes in the same way.

Using Images as Links

Images are good for more than just looks. You can use them to provide creative hyperlinks to other documents. HTML makes this easy because using an image as a link is exactly the same as using text. You are still using the anchor tag (the <a> tag you learned about in Lesson 4, "Linking Text and Documents") to surround the item you want to act as the hyperlink to another document. When you link from an image, the anchor tags must surround the image tag. Following is an example of the HTML you would use:

```
<a href="DOC2.htm">
<img src="images\happyFace.jpg" alt="Put on a happy face."
    height="60" width="60" />
</a>
```

When your visitors move their mouse pointers over the happyFace.jpg image in this sample, they will see a pop-up that says, "Put on a happy face." When the visitors click on the image, they will open the DOC2.htm file referenced by the anchor tag.

Thumbnail Images

Another popular use of the hyperlinking capability of HTML is to link from one image to another. Why would you want to do that? Well, many times the image you want to display is so large that it takes longer to load into the browser than you think people would like to wait. If that's so, you can create a smaller version of the file, called a *thumbnail*, that will load more quickly into the browser. The visitor simply clicks the thumbnail if he wants to open the larger file. Here's how it's done.

```
<a href="large_image.jpg">
<img src="thumbnail.jpg" alt="Click here to view a larger
    image." height="60" width="60" />
</a>
```

As you can see, clicking the thumbnail.jpg image will open another image (large_image.jpg). The alt attribute in this sample tells the visitor how to open the larger image.

 Tip   Many image editor programs provide tools to help you create thumbnail images of your large graphics. You can also use standalone products, such as Cerious Software's Thumbs Plus available at `ftp://ftp.cerious.com/pub/cerious/thmpls32.exe.`

Image Etiquette

Images are fun and colorful and easy to add to your HTML, but following are some etiquette rules to follow if you want your visitors to be happy with your site.

- The larger an image's file size, the longer it will take to load into the browser. Because most visitors to the World Wide Web still use a slow speed modem to connect, their time is precious. If you remember that and make sure to use small images whenever possible, you'll find that your visitors are happier.

- Not only is the file size of the individual image important, but also is the total file size of your HTML document. The more images you add—even small images—the larger your file size will become. Previewing your page in several browsers will help you determine how long your page will take to load in the browser. If you find the time too slow, so will your visitors.

- While the alt attribute is one of the most important attributes (because it should be used every time you use the <img /> tag), it pays to remember some simple guidelines. Make sure that the text for the `alt` attribute is relevant to the image—anything less will frustrate your visitors.

- On the subject of relevance: Be sure that your images are relevant to the text. An image of an airplane works great if you're talking about travel plans, but means nothing if you're talking about wildlife.

- You can find images all over the Internet, and saving them to your own computer for use later is easy (see the following Tip). Just as in the publishing world, however, graphic designers can protect their images by copyright. If you've found an image you like on a commercial Web site, look for a copyright notice or other legal statement that indicates whether the image is free for the taking. There are plenty of free images available on the Internet without using copyrighted material.

 Tip You can copy any Web image to your own computer, as long as it isn't protected by copyright. Just right-click on the image (or hold down the mouse button if you are on a Macintosh computer) and select Save Image As from the pop-up menu. Save the file on your own computer and use it as you would any other image file.

Table 8.2 lists the HTML tags that were discussed in this lesson.

Table 8.2   HTML Tags Used in This Lesson

HTML Tag	Closing	Description of Use
`<img src="location" />`		Adds an image to an HTML document.
`<object>`	`</object>`	Adds an object (can be used for images) to a HTML document.

In this lesson, you've learned:

- The two most frequently used graphics file formats found on the Web are GIF and JPEG. JPEG is used primarily for realistic, photographic-quality images; GIF is used for almost everything else. PNG is expected replace GIF soon.

- All images are added to HTML documents with the image tag and the source attribute, `<img src="location" />`.

- You can use the `<a>` tag to link an image to another document.

- Images are part of the fun of Web pages, but they are also part of the problem; large file sizes mean longer page load times.

LESSON 9
Mapping Images

In this lesson, you'll learn how to use image maps to link one image to many pages.

What Are Image Maps?

You've learned how to use an image to link to another page, but did you know that you can subdivide a single image and link each part of that image to another page? This type of subdivided image is called an *image map*.

> **Image map**   An image that is divided into pieces that are linked to (or, mapped to) more than one resource, such as an HTML page, a file, or another image.

You've probably seen image maps on the Web, even if you didn't know what they were. Rather than creating a different image for each button in the navigation bar, many Web designers create a single image that contains all the buttons and then use image maps to link each button to the appropriate page. Look at the following examples:

- The Amazon Web site (www.amazon.com) also uses image maps to create their navigation bar.

- The navigation bar on the CDNOW Web site (www.cdnow.com) also is created using an image map.

- The region map on the Society of Technical Communications Web site (http://www.stc.org/region_info.html) is created using an image map.

FIGURE 9.1   This image has been subdivided into four parts (one for each button on my navigation bar). Notice that some pieces of the image will not be linked to anything. Do not draw the boxes on your own image; I did it for demonstration purposes.

Finding the Coordinates

Like any other map, image maps have coordinates. In an image map, the coordinates, which are written as pixels, mark the corners of the piece of the image that will be linked to a specific URL. Before you can create any image map, you have to know the coordinates for your image.

Many image editors are available that can help you determine these coordinates and give them to you in a file so that you can cut and paste them into your HTML document. However, it's a lot easier to let your image editor do the work for you. Just type "create image map" into your favorite Web search engine to find several programs.

If you want to create your own image map, use the image editor to find the coordinates, write them down, and add those coordinates to your HTML file. Figure 9.2 shows you how Paint Shop Pro displays the coordinates for an image. I highlighted the portion of my navigation bar that I wanted to map to my home page and Paint Shop Pro told me which coordinates to use. As the figure shows, the highlighted section is a rectangle with corners at −1, 107 and 189, 167.

Caution   You can divide your image into rectangular, circular, or irregular polygon shapes. The rectangle is the easiest shape to use when you're getting started and that's the shape used in Figure 9.2.

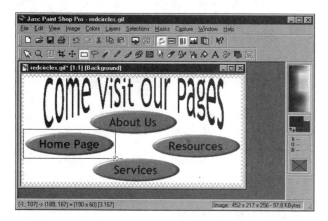

FIGURE 9.2   Paint Shop Pro displays the coordinates of a selected region of the image in the lower-left corner.

 Caution   The pixel coordinates for an image mark the corners of the portion of the image you are highlighting. The coordinates are relative to the entire image, not to the position of the image on the Web page. Use your image editor to gather the coordinates and you won't get confused.

Client-Side Versus Server-Side

With HTML, you can create image maps that work on the client-side and the server-side. The following list indicates the differences:

- *Client-side*   When you click on a client-side image map, the Web browser does all the work to bring you to the new location. The browser selects the link that was specified for the activated region and follows it.

- *Server-side*   When you click on a server-side image map, the server that stores the map interprets the commands and brings you to the page to which you are linked.

So how do you know which one to use? Most Web page authors only use client-side image maps because they are faster and anyone with a version 3.0 browser or higher can view them. You can always provide text links for older browsers that don't recognize the client-side image maps. Because client-side image mapping is the type of image map used most often, it is the one you'll learn about in the following section.

 Tip   When you are planning your Web page design, remember that you might not need to use an image map at all. You can place several smaller images close together for the same look. As long as the areas you want to link are primarily rectangular, this process is very easy with HTML and the <img> tag you learned in Lesson 8, "Adding Images."

Creating Client-Side Image Maps

Let's get started. After you have an image and have determined the coordinates for each piece of the image, you can begin mapping your image in HTML. The following HTML sample shows the image map I created for the navigation bar shown in Figure 9.1:

```
<!DOCTYPE html
     PUBLIC "-//W3C//DTD XHTML 1.0 Transitional//EN"
     "DTD/xhtml1-transitional.dtd">
<html xmlns="http://www.w3.org/1999/xhtml"
     xml:lang="en" lang="en">
<head>
```

```
<title>Image Maps</title>
<style type="text/css">
body {text-align="center"}
</style>
</head>
<body>
<map name="NavBar" id="NavBar">
<area shape="rect" coords="270, 91, 416, 138"
      href="resources.htm" alt="resources" " />
<area shape="rect" coords="139, 117, 287, 166"
      href="services.htm" alt="services" "" />
<area shape="rect" coords ="139, 61, 290, 111"
      href="about.htm" alt="about us" />
<area shape="rect" coords ="5, 84, 157, 139"
      href="default.htm" alt="home page" />
</map>
<img src="redcircles.jpg" width="424" height="166"
     alt="My Nav Bar" border="0" usemap="#NavBar" />
</body>
</html>
```

Look at the HTML example for image maps a little closer:

- `<map name="x" id="x">` Every image map needs a name and an id. It works just like the named anchor tag `<a>` you saw in Lesson 4, "Linking Text and Documents." It identifies the section of the HTML document that you want to reference from your image.

- `<area shape="w" coords="x" href="y" alt="z" />` An `<area />` tag is required for each portion of an image that will be linked. It identifies the shape of that portion, the coordinates for it, and the URL to which it will lead.

- `</map>` This tag closes the preceding `<map name>` tag.

- `usemap="#Map Name"` usemap is an attribute of the `<img />` tag. It points the Web browser to the correct image map for this image. Notice the # sign that precedes the map name; it works just like creating a hyperlink to a named anchor within the current document.

The Web browser sees the image map and knows that the image will be linked. In Figure 9.3, you can see that the mouse pointer changes into a hand when it hovers over a portion of the image that is mapped, as it does when placed over any other hyperlink.

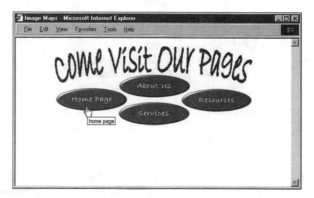

FIGURE 9.3   The image from Figure 9.2 displayed in the Web browser. Notice that the mouse pointer changes into a hand when it hovers over a mapped portion of the image.

Adding Text Links for Older Browsers

Because client-side image maps can only be interpreted by version 3.0 or later Web browsers, you'll need to provide another way for your visitors to get to the other pages in your Web site. The easiest way to do this is to provide text links under your image, as shown in the following HTML sample and in Figure 9.4:

```
<img src="redcircles.jpg" width="424" height="166"
     alt="My Nav Bar" usemap="#NavBar" />
<p align="center" />
<a href="default.htm">Home Page</a> |
<a href="about.htm">About Us</a> |
<a href="resources.htm">Resources</a> |
<a href="services.htm">Services</a>
```

As you can see, text links are standard HTML <a href> links. They will follow the <img /> tag and direct the viewer to the same pages they could reach with the image map. Figure 9.4 shows you how these links will look in the Web browser.

FIGURE 9.4   The image from Figure 9.2 displayed in the Web browser, with additional text links provided for older browsers.

Creating a Separate Map File

If you find it easier to keep track of a separate file, you could also create your image map in a separate file that includes the image maps for all your pages. In the following example, I created a separate file, called map.htm:

```
<!DOCTYPE html
     PUBLIC "-//W3C//DTD XHTML 1.0 Transitional//EN"
     "DTD/xhtml1-transitional.dtd">
<html xmlns="http://www.w3.org/1999/xhtml"
     xml:lang="en" lang="en">
<head>
<title>Image Maps</title>
<style type=""text/css"">
</style>
</head>
<body>
<map name="NavBar" id="NavBar">
<area shape="rect" coords="270, 91, 416, 138"
     href="services.htm" alt="services" />
<area shape="rect" coords="139, 117, 287, 166"
     href="resources.htm" alt="resources" />
```

```
<area shape="rect" coords="139, 61, 290, 111"
      href="about.htm" alt="about" />
<area shape="rect" coords="5, 84, 157, 139"
      href="default.htm" alt="home page" />
</map>
</body>
</html>
```

Notice that this file includes all of the information associated with the image map we created in the previous examples (everything between the `<map name>` and `</map>` tags), but it does not include an `<img />` tag. The `<img />` tag (with a `usemap` attribute that points to my image map file) would be included in another Web page, as shown in the following sample.

```
<!DOCTYPE html
      PUBLIC "-//W3C//DTD XHTML 1.0 Transitional//EN"
      "DTD/xhtml1-transitional.dtd">
<html xmlns="http://www.w3.org/1999/xhtml"
      xml:lang="en" lang="en">
<head>
<title>Another Web Page</title>
<style type="text/css">
body {text-align:"center"}
</style>
</head>
<body>
<img src="redcircles.jpg" width="424" height="166"
      alt="My Nav Bar" border="0" usemap="map.htm/#NavBar" />
</body>
</html>
```

In the preceding Web page sample, the `usemap` attribute of the `<img />` tag now includes the name of the file that holds the NavBar image map (map.htm).

Table 9.1 lists the HTML tags that were discussed in this lesson.

Table 9.1   HTML Tags Used in This Lesson

HTML Tag	Closing	Description of Use
`<area />`		Identifies the shape (`circle`, `rect`, or `poly`), coordinates (in pixels), and URL for each section of the image.
`<map name>`	`</map>`	Surrounds the image map and gives a reference name to be used with the `usemap="#map name"` attribute.

In this lesson, you've learned:

- Image maps link a single image to multiple Internet resources. The most popular examples of image maps on the Web are for navigation bars.

- Paint Shop Pro and other graphics programs enable you to create your image, *and* determine the coordinates for the image map.

- Image maps can be contained within your HTML document or in a separate file.

Lesson 10
Creating Frames

In this lesson, you'll learn to create frames. You'll also learn why some people don't like them and how you can use them effectively.

Simple Frames

HTML *frames* give you a way to display two or more HTML documents at once. Each frame in the browser window displays its own HTML document. Those documents can link to each other or remain completely separate entities.

> **Frame** A complete HTML document that appears inside of, or alongside, one or more other HTML documents within the same browser window.

Most often, as in Figure 10.1, you'll see frames used as a navigation bar on a Web site. The navigation frame can appear on any edge of the document, but you'll probably find it on the top or left margins because English (the language of most Web pages) is oriented from top to bottom and left to right.

To create frames, you'll need to create a new type of HTML document, called a frameset. A *frameset* is a special type of HTML document that defines how many frames will be displayed and which HTML documents will appear in each frame. The frameset document for the page is displayed in Figure 10.1.

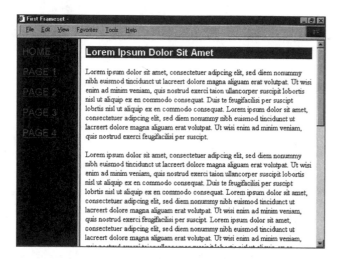

FIGURE 10.1   A simple two-frame document as it appears in the browser. The left frame contains the site's navigation bar and the right frame contains the pages to which the navigation buttons link.

```
<!DOCTYPE html
    PUBLIC "-//W3C//DTD XHTML 1.0 Frameset//EN"
    "DTD/xhtml1-frameset.dtd">
<html xmlns="http://www.w3.org/1999/xhtml"
    xml:lang="en" lang="en">
<head>
<title>First Frameset</title>
<style type="text/css">
</style>
</head>
<frameset cols="20%,*">
<frame src="toc.htm" name="left" id="left" />
<frame src="latin.htm" name="main" id="main" />
  <noframes>
    <body>
    <p><a href="toc.htm">Table of Contents</a></p>
    </body>
  </noframes>
</frameset>
</html>
```

> **Tip**   Did you notice that the <!DOCTYPE> tag changed? In Lesson 2, "Creating Your First Page," you learned that XHTML has three variations. The frameset variation is used whenever you create framed pages.

If you compare this document with a regular HTML document, you should notice right away that the <body> tag is missing. A frameset document uses a new tag, <frameset>, to replace the <body> tag. Within the <frameset> tag, you'll see the <frame /> tag, which is used to describe the contents of each frame, and the <noframes> tag, which is used to instruct the browser what to display in the event the viewer's browser does not support frames, including adding the <body> tag again. Confused? Let's take a closer look at each of these tags.

<frameset>

Within the <frameset> tag, you will need to define the orientation of the frames—in vertical columns, cols, or in horizontal rows, rows. This orientation attribute also requires you to define the size of each of your frames. For example, if you have three vertical frames in your frameset, you will need to specify three size attributes. Look again at the <frameset> tag in the preceding HTML sample.

```
<frameset cols="20%,*">
```

This tag defines two vertical columns. The first column is 20 percent of the screen width; the second column fills the remainder of the screen—80 percent. The asterisk (*) tells the browser to fill the remainder of the screen. You can use the same trick if you are defining more than two frames. Although it shows only two values, the following <frameset> tag will actually be used to define *three* horizontal rows. The first row has been set to 20 percent of the length of the screen; the asterisk forces the browser to equally divide the remainder of the screen between the other two rows.

```
<frameset rows="20%,*">
```

You don't have to let the browser figure out the size of your frames. If you are a perfectionist, you can do your own math and specify the size yourself. Just remember that the total value of the sizes can't be more than 100 percent of the screen. Now that makes sense, doesn't it?

Tip   You can specify the size of your frames in pixels or as a percentage of the browser window by using the % sign as in the following tag:

```
<frameset cols="50%,50%">.
```

You don't have to use the % sign, however. You can use a forward slash (/) as an abbreviation of the % sign, as in the following tag:

```
<frameset cols="50/,50/">.
```

`<frame />`

Like the `<img />` tag you learned about in Lesson 8, "Adding Images," the `<frame />` tag uses the `src` (source) attribute to tell the browser where to find the document to display. The important thing to remember when you are setting up your frameset document is that you are defining the start page for your Web site, or the first framed page in your site. You don't have to figure out every possible combination of pages that might appear, you only have to specify the first one.

The `<frame />` tag also requires the `name` and `id` attributes. Most people name their frames by their location on the browser window. The `<frame />` tags in the following example, for instance, call the frame that appears on the left of the screen, `left`, and the other frame `main` because it will hold the main pages of the Web site.

```
<frame src="toc.htm" name="left" id="left" />
<frame src="latin.htm" name="main" id="main" />
```

Tip You could name the frames anything (Dog, Cat, Red, or Blue), but you'll find them easier to remember if you stick to the basics.

Following are a few more attributes of the `<frame />` tag that might come in handy:

- `frameborder` With this attribute, you can remove the small border line that separates borders. In Figure 10.2, the border has been removed from the sample frameset.

- `marginwidth` or `marginheight` These attributes specify (in pixels) the space between the border and the text in the frame.

- `scrolling` Using the values of `yes`, `no`, or `auto`, you can tell the browser whether or not to add a scrollbar next to the frame. Don't worry, however; even if you've specified `scrolling="no"`, the browser will display a scrollbar if the content of the frame exceeds the size of the frame.

- `noresize` Just like any other window, you can resize frames manually by dragging the frame's border (even when the `frameborder="0"` attribute has been specified). You can avoid that by specifying the `noresize` attribute in your frameset.

`<noframes>`

The `<noframes>` tag that appears in the preceding example tells the browser what to do if it doesn't know how to display frames, or if your visitor has adjusted his browser's settings to refuse frames.

```
<noframes>
<body>
<p><a href="toc.htm">Table of Contents</a></p>
</body>
</noframes>
```

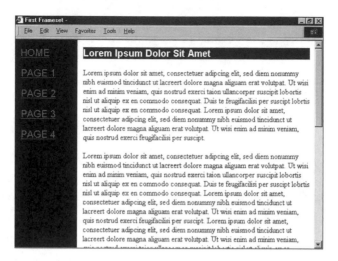

FIGURE 10.2   Figure 10.1 with the frameborder attribute set to "0".

The <noframes> tag is not required and many Web page authors choose to ignore it, but it takes very little effort to add it and it makes good sense if you want to be certain that everyone will be able to view your Web site.

While it's true that many authors ignore the <noframes> tag, you'll find that just as many authors choose to create an entire nonframed version of their Web site. I happen to think that's overkill.

If you are using frames as a navigation bar, you could make a couple simple changes to your main HTML pages to help people who can't see the frames navigate your site. In Figure 10.3, I've made the same frameset document from Figure 10.1 work for people who can't see frames. By adding a simple one-row table to hold a duplicate set of navigation elements, someone who stumbles upon your page, but can't see the frame on the left can still navigate the site.

FIGURE 10.3   Adding a navigation bar to the top of each of the main pages will make this site work for those people who can't view framed pages.

Nested Frames

You might want to be more creative with your frame layout. You can use the <frameset> tag more than once in a single frameset document. This feature enables you to nest frames within each other. Following is an example of a nested frame. I indented the second <frameset> to make it easier to read.

```
<!DOCTYPE html
    PUBLIC "-//W3C//DTD XHTML 1.0 Frameset//EN"
    "DTD/xhtml1-frameset.dtd">
<html xmlns="http://www.w3.org/1999/xhtml"
    xml:lang="en" lang="en">
<head>
<title>First Frameset</title>
<style type="text/css">
</style>
</head>
<frameset rows="15%,*,10%">
<frame src="sitename.htm" name="top" id="top" />
```

```
<frameset cols="20%,*,11%">
    <frame src="toc.htm" name="left" id="left" />
    <frame src="latin.htm" name="main" id="main" />
    <frame src="motto.htm" name="right" id="right" />
</frameset>
<frame src="contacts.htm" name="bottom" id="bottom" />
    <noframes>
        <body>
        <p><a href="toc.htm">Table of Contents</a></p>
        </body>
    </noframes>
</frameset>
</html>
```

The first <frameset> tag defines three horizontal frames, but the second
<frameset> tag divides the middle row into three column frames. Figure
10.4 shows you how this nested frameset will appear in the browser.

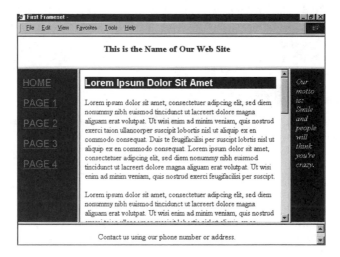

FIGURE **10.4**   All the borders have been left showing to help you
see where the nested frames are in this example.

<iframe>

You can create a frame one more way by using the <iframe>, or inline frame, tag. Rather than creating a separate frameset document, you define an inline frame within a regular HTML document because it appears in the middle of another document. Figure 10.5 shows the same content as the sample in Figure 10.4, but this page was created using an inline frame. You can see the HTML document for this page in Figure 10.6.

You can apply all the same attributes for regular frames to the <iframe> tag except the noresize attribute, because unlike regular frames, inline frames cannot be resized.

 Caution   As of right now, the <iframe> tag only works with Internet Explorer 4 and higher browsers, so don't try to use it unless you know your audience has that browser.

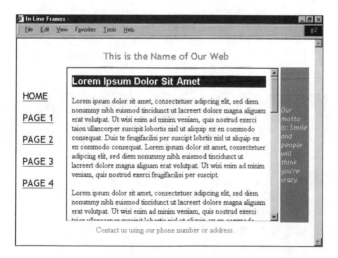

FIGURE 10.5   The scrollable document in the center of this page was added with an inline frame.

FIGURE 10.6 Style sheet properties are used to help define the colors and fonts for this document. The <iframe> tag is actually embedded inside a table to achieve the page layout shown in Figure 10.5.

Tip Throughout the book, you have been cautioned that not all browsers support all the HTML tags you've learned. For a fee, StatMarket tracks browser usage and other fun statistics on its Web site (http://www.statmarket.com). You can use that knowledge to decide whether you are willing to take the risk of using a tag such as <iframe>, which is not supported by all browsers.

Linking Between Frames

Think back to Lesson 4, "Linking Text and Documents," when you learned how to create hyperlinks. You'll remember that you can use the `<a name="x" id="x">` tag to name an anchor, or target, within a document that could be linked to directly, as shown in the following code.

```
<a name="PointA" id="PointA">Point A</a>
```

You'll remember that you need to use the anchor tag, `<a href="url#anchor">`, to surround the text that you want to highlight, as shown in the following example:

```
<a href="DOC2.htm#PointA">Click Here to go to Point A</a>
```

All frames have also have the `name` and `id` attributes assigned to them. You can use that name to specify which frame you want your hyperlink to open in. Let's look at the HTML code for the toc.htm file used in the preceding examples.

```
<!DOCTYPE html
     PUBLIC "-//W3C//DTD XHTML 1.0 Frameset//EN"
     "DTD/xhtml1-frameset.dtd">
<html xmlns="http://www.w3.org/1999/xhtml"
     xml:lang="en" lang="en">

<head>
<title>Table of Contents</title>
<style type="text/css">
</style>
</head>
<body>
<p><a href="homepage.htm" target="main">HOME</a></p>
<p><a href="page1.htm" target="main">Page 1</a></p>
<p><a href="page2.htm" target="main">Page 2</a></p>
<p><a href="page3.htm" target="main">Page 3</a></p>
<p><a href="page4.htm" target="main">Page 4</a></p>
</body>
</html>
```

Now you see a new attribute has been attached to the `<a href>` tag: target. The `target` attribute refers to the *target frame* for the hyperlink. Besides the frame names that you've specified in your frameset document, you can target the following other three names:

- `<a href="url" target="blank">` This tag opens the hyperlink in a new browser window.

- `<a href="url" target="self">` This tag opens the hyperlink in the same window where the hyperlink was. If the hyperlink was in a frame, the link will open in the same frame, replacing that frame document.

- `<a href="url" target="top">` This tag opens the hyperlink in the same browser window. If the hyperlink was in a frame, the link will open in the same frame, replacing the entire frameset.

Target Frame The name of the frame in which a hyperlink will open.

 Caution Always specify the `target` attribute whenever you are working with frames. If you don't specify the target frame, the browser generally will replace the current frame with the target document, which probably is not what you'd intended.

The Two Biggest Problems with Frames

Mention frames to any Web site developer, and you'll be sure to get an earful. Good or bad, people always have an opinion. You've already seen how useful they can be at providing navigation information, but let's see why so many people dislike them.

Tip Jakob Nielsen, one of the Web's most respected usability experts, maintains a Web page called (and pardon my French), Why Frames Suck (Most of the Time), in which he discusses some of the many problems users have with frames. You can read his original 1996 article at www.useit.com/alertbox/9612.html, which was later updated in 1999 (http://www.useit.com/alertbox/990502.html).

So Many Pages, So Few URLs

When you load your frameset document into your browser, you are telling the browser to load all the pages into this same document, following the selected hyperlinks. So? Take a look at the URL for your frameset document. My URL is C:\Webshare\wwwroot\sams\frame2.htm. No matter how many times I click the hyperlinks in my framed pages, the URL stays the same because all those framed pages are loading into the same frameset document.

Why is that a problem? Suppose that my best customer is browsing my site and she is looking at the *wonderful* information on Page4.htm. She decides to save the URL in her Favorites (or bookmark it) so that she doesn't have to search for the information again. The URL she saves is C:\Webshare\wwwroot\sams_frame2.htm, not C:\Webshare\wwwroot\sams\page4.htm, which is what she was actually looking at. There is no guarantee that when she opens that URL in the browser, it will open on Page4.htm, as she wanted in the first place. How frustrating!

If you right-click the mouse (or hold the mouse button if you have a Macintosh), you can click Properties in the shortcut menu. On the Properties dialog box is the URL for that particular page (see Figure 10.7). You can highlight and copy that URL into the Address field of your browser to open later. When you do this, however, you will not see the framed version of the site; you will only see the single document that you saved, with no additional navigation to help you.

Figure 10.7   The Properties dialog box contains the actual URL for a framed page. You can copy the URL using the shortcut menu after you highlight the text.

Printing

Another huge problem for users of your framed Web site is *printing*. Why should printing be a problem? As much as we like to think that we are headed toward paperless offices and online commerce, people still like to print documents. When most people see a page that they want to print, they click the Print button on their browser. With frames, the Print button only prints the *active frame*.

Active Frame   The last frame that you clicked.

On my sample framed site, if you clicked a link in the left frame to open a new document in the main frame and then clicked the Print button without making any other mouse clicks, you would actually print the navigation bar on the left frame, not the document in the main frame that you wanted. Unfortunately, the browser doesn't know which frame you want, only which frame was last active.

The newer browser versions have included a new feature in their Print dialog boxes—a Print Frames option that allows you to specify whether you want to print the active frame or the entire frameset (see Figure 10.8). That's an improvement, but it requires extra clicks (and some know-how).

FIGURE 10.8   The Print dialog box from Internet Explorer.

    Tip   If you want to print a single frame, you can click the right-mouse button, or hold down the mouse button if you are using a Macintosh, and select the Print option from the shortcut menu. The printer will print only the selected frame, not the entire frameset.

Using Frames Effectively

Although frames have some usability problems, there are some obvious advantages for using them. Just make sure that you use them the right way. Here are some tips to help.

- *Frames are not a toy*   Frames work best when used as a navigation tool, or when it makes sense to show two or more elements of a document at the same time.

- *Remember the target attribute*   Nothing is worse than clicking a hyperlink in a framed document and break out of frames unintentionally. Worse, each hyperlink in a framed document that does not include the `target` attribute has the potential of opening in a new browser window. You could end up with a real mess.

- *Include the* <noframes> *tag*   Always remember that there are people who can't see frames (either because of older browsers, or because they set their browser preferences to ignore them). Provide alternate content with the <noframes> tag.

- *Include alternate navigation within the main frame*   With the Web, there is no guarantee that your visitors will always arrive at your home page and see the frameset as you intended them to see it. Sometimes, they will arrive on an individual frame. If you provide additional navigation links within those pages, your visitors will still be able to move within your site.

- *Never frame other framed pages*   Not as frequent anymore on the Web, but when frames first became available, Web page authors framed everything, including other framesets. This compound-framing is very confusing to users.

Table 10.1   HTML Tags Used in This Lesson

HTML Tag	Closing	Description of Use
<a href>	</a>	Creates hyperlinks to other documents. Always use the target attribute with frames.
<frameset>	</frameset>	Replaces the <body> tag in a frameset document and surrounds the <frame> and <noframes> tags. This tag must include the attribute to describe the orientation of the frames and their size.
<frame />		Includes the frame's name and id and a URL for the content (src). It also might include attributes to define the border and scrolling.

Table 10.1 Continued

HTML Tag	Closing	Description of Use
<iframe>	</iframe>	Embeds a frame inside another document. It only works with Internet Explorer.
<noframes>	</noframes>	Defines an alternate viewing page for browsers that don't support frames.

In this lesson, you've learned:

- A frameset document defines the number of frames and their sizes; standard HTML documents will be contained in the frames.

- Each frame of a frameset document must be named so that you can direct your hyperlink to appear in a specific *target* frame.

- Despite their obvious advantage for organizing your site's navigation elements, many people dislike frames because of usability problems associated with them.

LESSON 11
Creating Forms

In this lesson, you'll learn how to create Web forms that enable you to get input from your visitors.

Creating Forms

You've seen forms on the Web, but I'll bet you didn't know they were so easy to create. I want to point out a couple of things for you to keep track of as you read this section and then you'll create a form.

- Forms are made up of fields (that you want the user to fill out) and buttons (to perform actions such as submit and reset).

- Every field (<input type="type" />) should have name and id attributes as well.

- Every field can be set to have a default value (a pre-selected option that the users can overwrite if they want); many also can be set to validate the data the user enters.

- Every form requires a submit button that sends the form data to the address specified in the action attribute of the <form> tag. It has its own <input /> tag and you can read more about it in the "Buttons" section later in this lesson.

One more thing: A form isn't a form until it is enclosed within the <form> tag. The <form> tag always includes an action and a method attribute. To make it simple, a form's method is almost always set to *post* and the `action` can only be one of two values: an e-mail address of the person who will be receiving the form's data, or a URL of a file that will be receiving the form's data. We're going to use the e-mail option because it's easier for you to practice with. Following is a simple `<form>` tag, but Figure 11.2 shows the full HTML document, including the `<form>` tag, for the form shown in Figure 11.1.

```
<form method="mailto:youremail@yourisp.com" action="post">
```

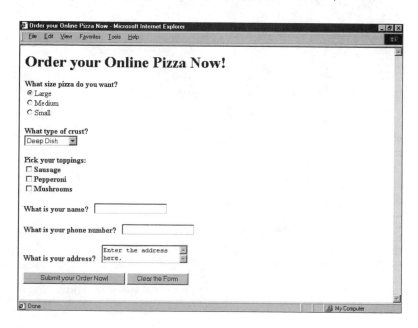

FIGURE 11.1   This Web form contains each of the input types (fields) available.

Don't forget that an HTML form is just like any other HTML document; it doesn't recognize extra spaces. If you want to line up your fields for a more professional looking form, line up your form fields in tables, as shown in Figure 11.3, and use style sheet properties to define your fonts and add images.

```
pizza.txt - Notepad
File  Edit  Search  Help
<html xmlns="http://www.w3.org/1999/xhtml"
      xml:lang="en" lang="eng">
<html>
<head>
<title>Order your Online Pizza Now</title>
<style type="text/css">
</style>
</head>
<body>
<h1>Order your Online Pizza Now!</h1>
<form action="mailto:youremail@yourisp.com" method="POST">
<p><strong>What size pizza would you like?</strong><br />
  <input type="radio" value="large" name="size" id="size" checked />Large<br />
  <input type="radio" value="med" name="size" id="size" />Medium<br />
  <input type="radio" value="small" name="size" id="size" />Small<br />
<p><strong>What type of crust?</strong><br />
  <select name="crust" id="crust" size="1">
    <option value="Deep Dish" selected>Deep Dish</option>
    <option value="Hand-Tossed">Hand-Tossed</option>
    <option value="Thin &amp; Crispy">Thin &amp; Crispy</option>
  </select></p>
<p><strong>Pick your toppings:</strong><br />
  <input type="checkbox" name="toppings" id="toppings" value="sausage" />Sausage<br />
  <input type="checkbox" name="toppings" id="toppings" value="pepperoni" />Pepperoni<br />
  <input type="checkbox" name="toppings" id="toppings" value="mushrooms" />Mushrooms</p>
<p><strong>What is your name?</strong> 
  <input type="text" name="name" id="name" size="20" /><br />
<p><strong>What is your phone number?</strong> 
  <input type="text" name="phone" id="phone" size="20" /><br />
<p><strong>What is your address?</strong> 
  <textarea name="address" id="address" rows="2" cols="20">Enter the address here.</textarea>
<p><input type="submit" name="submit" id="submit" value="Submit your Order Now!" >
  <input type="reset" name="reset" id="reset" value="Clear the Form"></p>
</form>
</body>
```

FIGURE 11.2   Here's the HTML document for the form shown in Figure 11.1.

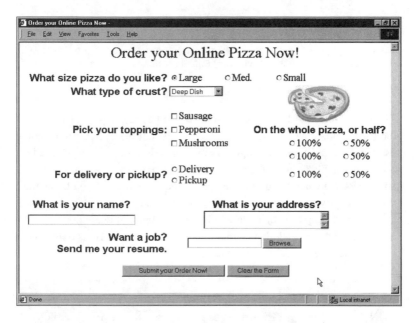

FIGURE **11.3**   This version of the form took a little longer to create, but the results are worth it.

Form Fields

The main reason to create a form is to collect data. The fields on a form help you do that. The following sections describe each of the field types and give you some hints for how each one can be customized to suit your needs.

Text Box

The simplest form of data collection is an empty box. Your form poses a question ("What is your name?") and your visitor fills in the answer in the space provided. In HTML, this type of field is called a text box. HTML uses the <input /> command to identify a form field. The following example is a complete HTML form with one field—a text box—that is 40 pixels wide and is called *Name*.

```
<form action="mailto:youremail@yourisp.com" method="post">
<p><b>What is your name?</b></p>
<p><input type="text" name="Name" id="Name" size="40" /></p>
<p><input type="submit" value="Submit" name="submit"
id="submit" /></p>
</form>
```

The form field's attributes (type, name, id, and size) help to customize the form field. Name, id, and size are obvious, but the type attribute could use some explanation. Although this type of field traditionally is called a *text* box, you also can set the type attribute to password (which displays an asterisk (*) when the user types his or her password). If you know that your visitors will be using Internet Explorer, you could also set the type attribute to integer (which is a whole number without decimals) or number (which can include decimals). One more type, file, is explained in the "File Select" section found later.

 Tip The tabindex attribute, shown within the <input /> tags on Figure 11.2, sets the order in which the user can navigate through the form elements using the Tab key. The tabindex attribute and the index number increases toward the bottom of the form.

Text Area

You use the <textarea> tag to define a multiline text box. In addition to the usual name, id, and tabindex attributes, all <textarea> boxes should control the size of the box using the rows and cols attributes. cols indicates the width of the field in pixels; rows indicates the height of the field.

Anything you type between the <textarea> and </textarea> tags will appear inside the field and can be overwritten by users when they are completing the form. The following example shows the code for a text area box with an initial value of "Enter the address here."

```
<textarea name="address" id="address"
        rows="2" cols"20" tabindex="10">Enter
        the address here.</textarea>
```

Radio Buttons and Check Boxes

Radio button and check box fields are very similar. In fact, there's really only one difference between them: Your user can select only one item in a radio button list, but can select multiple check box items. Look at the form in Figure 11.1 again. Check boxes are used for the pizza toppings question because it is possible that your visitors might want multiple toppings. Radio buttons are used to ask about the preferred size of the pizza because only one pizza at a time can be ordered with this form.

The following example demonstrates how a check box field is created. Notice all the check box fields that relate to the same question ("Pick your toppings") have the same name and id attributes. You use the value attribute to specify the information you will see when the form data is submitted to you. If you don't specify any value, the form data typically will send on/off or yes/no values for all fields.

```
<p><input type="checkbox" name="toppings" id="toppings"
value="sausage" /> Sausage<br />
<input type="checkbox" name="toppings" id="toppings"
value="pepperoni" /> Pepperoni<br />
<input type="checkbox" name="toppings" id="toppings"
value="mushrooms" /> Mushrooms</p>
```

With radio buttons, you'll need to use the checked attribute to set a starting value for each field. When you do specify a preselected option, be sure to select the most frequently submitted value. In the following example, the large pizza has been preselected. Users can change that selection when they are completing the form and the form data will be submitted to you with the users' choices selected.

```
<p><input type="radio" value="large" name="size"
        id="size" checked />Large<br />
<input type="radio" value="med" name="size" id="size" />
Medium<br />
<input type="radio" value="small" name="size" id="size" />
Small</p>
```

Drop-down Option

The drop-down menu option, shown in the following HTML sample, uses a <select> tag to define the overall menu (such as giving it a name, id,

and a `size`—the number of rows visible at any time). Enclosed within the
`<select>` tag are `<option>` tags that describe the contents of the drop-
down menu. As with radio buttons, you can specify a start value for the
drop-down menu using the `selected` attribute.

```
<select name="crust" id="crust" size="1">
   <option value="Deep Dish" selected>Deep Dish</option>
   <option value="Hand-Tossed">Hand-Tossed</option>
   <option value="Thin &amp; Crispy">Thin &amp; Crispy</option>
</select>
```

 Tip Some form designers like to add an `<option>` tag
at the top of their drop-down menu fields that tells
their users to select one of the items from the list. The
drop-down menu field in Figure 11.4 demonstrates
this option.

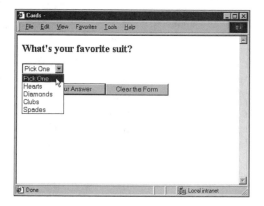

FIGURE 11.4 This drop-down menu includes an extra `<option>` tag
for the Pick One statement.

Like check boxes, your user can select multiple options in the drop-down
menu by adding the `multiple` attribute to the `<select>` tag. This change
(shown in the following HTML sample) enables users to select multiple

options by pressing and holding down the CTRL key while clicking on the options in the menu. (See Figure 11.5.)

```
<form action="mailto:youremail@yourisp.com" method="post">
<h3>What's your favorite card suit(s)?</h3>
<select name="suit" id="suit" size="2" multiple="multiple">
    <option value="Hearts">Hearts</option>
    <option value="Diamonds">Diamonds</option>
    <option value="Clubs">Clubs</option>
    <option value="Spades">Spades</option>
</select>
```

FIGURE 11.5   Setting a `size="2"` attribute in this drop-down menu enables the visitor to see two options at once. Here, both options have been selected.

File Select

Another useful way to gather information from your visitors is to allow them to send you files. You might use this input option, the `file` type, to collect résumés, orders, or any other type of file. The following HTML sample demonstrates how this option is created. As you can see in Figure 11.6, the browser creates a Browse button to help your visitors send their files.

```
<form action="mailto:youremail@yourisp.com" method="post">
<p>Send me your resume.</p>
<p><input type="file" enctype="multipart/form-data"
        name="resume" id="resume" /></p>
<p><input type="submit" value="send now"
        name="submit" id="submit" /></p>
</form>
```

FIGURE 11.6 The visitor will press the Browse button to browse their own file system in search of the appropriate file.

 Caution Check with your Web host before creating this type of form; they might have additional requirements for you.

Buttons

The Submit and Reset buttons are special types of form elements. Although they are created using the <input /> tag (see Figure 11.2), they are not data collection tools, but actually are data submission tools.

- The Submit button collects all the data from the form and *posts* (sends) it to the location specified in the action portion of the <form> tag.

- The Reset button clears the form of any data that might have already been completed. The Reset button *resets* the form to the original preselected values.

The Submit button is required on all forms, but the Reset button is optional. The browser's Refresh button has the same effect as the Reset button on a form. It reloads the page and deletes everything except the initial values of the form.

 Tip There is one more input type to be aware of: the hidden type. A hidden field is not displayed on the form, but returns results anyway. You might want to collect the date and time the visitor submitted the form, the version of the form that was submitted, or the name of the person who should receive the data. Create the field based on the HTML example that follows.

```
<input type="hidden" name="version"
       id="version" value="B" />
```

Receiving Form Data

When your visitors click the Submit button on a form on your Web site, the data they entered into the form will be sent to you using the action you specified in your <form> tag. In Figure 11.2, we selected an e-mail action. Figure 11.7 shows you how my e-mail software returns the form data to me. You should now see why it is so important to include the name and id attributes associated with every form field.

```
From: yourvisitor@hisisp.com
To: youremail@yourisp.com
Subject: Form

Size=Large
Crust=Deep Dish
Toppings=Pepperoni+Sausage
Name=your visitor's Name
Phone=your visitor's Phone number
Address=your visitor's Address
```

FIGURE 11.7 Your e-mail software may format the responses differently, but they will all show the field name (Size and Toppings, for example), along with the data your visitor entered into those fields.

It is not always convenient to receive form data via e-mail, particularly if you expect to receive a lot of responses. Reading, and responding to, that many e-mail messages can become tiresome. Your ISP also might prefer that you do not use its mail servers in this manner.

Another action that you can assign to your forms is a script to handle the responses for you. Scripts are automated form handlers and can be used to collect all the responses in a single file and respond to the visitors for you. This book can't begin to explain how to write the scripts, or find them, but your ISP, or your network administrator, probably will have several scripts available for you to choose from and can help you attach them to your form. The important thing to remember is "Ask."

Table 11.1 lists the HTML tags that were discussed in this lesson.

Table 11.1   HTML Tags Used in This Lesson

HTML Tag	Closing	Description of Use
`<form>`	`</form>`	Encloses all form elements.
`<input />`		Identifies a form field.
`<option>`	`</option>`	Identifies the contents of a drop menu.
`<select>`	`</select>`	Encloses a drop-down menu field.
`<textarea>`	`</textarea>`	Identifies a multilined text field.

In this lesson, you've learned:

- All form fields should have name, id, and tabindex attributes.

- The `<form>` tag always includes a method attribute (which is usually post) and an action attribute. The action can be either an e-mail address or a URL of a file that will be receiving the form's data.

- The six form field types are text box, text area, radio buttons, check boxes, drop-down option menus, and the file browse box.

LESSON 12

Making It Sing: Sound and Other Multimedia

In this lesson, you'll learn how to add sound and video to your Web pages, and find the plug-ins required to use them.

Adding Sound and Video

Used correctly, sound and video clips can greatly enhance the content in your Web pages. Imagine a Web page about Dr. Martin Luther King, Jr. that didn't include something about his famous "I Have a Dream" speech. The text of the speech is moving, but the delivery is what made it so powerful. You can add sound and video clips to your own Web pages using some HTML tags you've already learned.

 Tip   You can hear samples of the "I Have a Dream" speech at http://www.wakeamerica.com/past/ speeches/1960/mking_082863.html.

Once again, however, you'll find that the three major players in the world of HTML can't agree on a method for adding something so powerful. This lesson discusses other methods for adding these sound and video clips. You should know that the one method that is sure to work with every browser on every platform is also the simplest: the <a> tag.

```
<a href="http://www.ibiblio.org/pub/multimedia/sun-sounds/
    screams/Scream.au">Hear the screams!</a>
```

When your visitors click on the words *Hear the screams!*, the scream.au file will download to their computers and begin playing. If the visitors do not have the correct plug-in to hear the sound clip, the browser should prompt them to save the file for later. It will not, however, prompt them to download the correct plug-in. You will need to do that on your page.

Tip   Try typing "sound clips" into your favorite search engine to find sound files you could use on your own pages.

Video clips can be handled in exactly the same way:

```
<a href="http://spaceflight.nasa.gov/realdata/sightings/
    skywatch2_28.asf">
    Learn about the SkyWatch Space Station program.</a>
```

Caution   Use sound and video sparingly and make the wait worthwhile. Even short clips can have a large file size and may take a very long time to load. Make sure that you give your visitors some idea of the content of the clip so that they can decide whether to wait for the download.

<embed>

Netscape invented a new tag called <embed> to enable you to include a sound or video clip on a Web page. Microsoft's Internet Explorer browser also accepts this nonstandard tag. The following sample shows how the <embed> tag works to add a video clip.

```
<p>Wonder what would happen if Rosie O'Donnell went on safari?
    Click the video to begin playing.</p>
    <embed src=" C:\webshare\wwwroot\videos\safari.asx"
```

```
                autostart="false" loop="false">
 <noembed>
 <a href="videos\safari.asx">Click_for a surprise.</a>
 </noembed>
<p>You will need the <a href="http://www.microsoft.com/
   windows/windowsmedia/en/download/default.asp"> Windows
   Media Player</a> to see this clip.</p>
</embed>
```

The browser displays a the control panel for the media device you use, as shown in Figure 12.1. You can add width and height attributes to the <embed> tag to control the size of the video still. The <noembed> tag provides an alternate way for visitors to download the video if their browser doesn't recognize the <embed> tag.

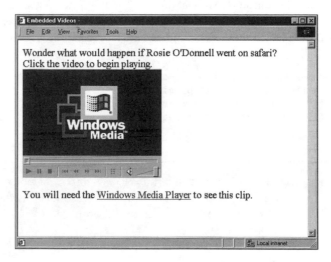

FIGURE 12.1 When embedded, a control panel for the device used to play the video or sound clip, appears in the browser.

Notice that I've included two attributes for the <embed> tag in this example: autostart and loop. Autostart, which you can set to true or false, tells the browser whether to begin playing the clip immediately upon loading the page. The loop attribute tells the browser how many times in a row to play the clip before stopping. You can set the `loop` attribute to any whole number.

Another attribute you can set is `autorewind`. This attribute is automatically set to `true`, but if for some reason you *don't* want to rewind the clip after it plays, you can set it to `false`. The `hidden` attribute hides the player's VCR controls from the user. Hiding the controls gives you, the developer, more control over the use of the clip, but may annoy your visitors if they are not allowed to turn your clip on or off.

`<object>`

The `<embed>` tag is nonstandard, which means that the W3C doesn't recognize it as a legitimate HTML markup tag. The W3C prefers that Web page developers include sound and video clips using the `<object>` tag. You will learn more about this tag in Lesson 14, "Creating Active Web Pages."

```
<p>Wonder what would happen if Rosie O'Donnell went on safari?
   Click the video to begin playing.</p>
<object classid="C:\webshare\wwwroot\videos\safari.asx">
<a href="C:\webshare\wwwroot\videos\safari.asx">Surprise!</a>
</object>
```

 Caution Unfortunately, the `<object>` tag does not yet work consistently in all browsers, although it is the W3C-preferred tagging method. Be prepared to either always include an alternate `<a href>` tag for sound and video elements, or duplicate your work by including the `<embed>` tag as well.

The `<object>` tag also comes with a multitude of attributes that you can set to help control the use of the clip in your Web page. You can add a border around the object by using the `appearance` attribute and setting the value to 1. The `<object>` tag also has an `autostart` and `autorewind` attribute.

Finding Plug-ins

We've mentioned before that it's never a good idea to include any items on your Web page that require a plug-in (such as Flash or RealAudio) without also providing a link to the plug-in. You don't want to assume that your visitors will have the required software to view your page because they might not.

Microsoft generally believes that the browser itself should contain enough code to run any scripts, applications, and embedded items without loading plug-ins, and it uses ActiveX controls to handle these types of events. Netscape, however, agrees with the idea that browsers should be light and plug-ins should be used to handle outside events. Partially because of this belief, Netscape maintains one of the best plug-in archives on the Web at `http://home.netscape.com/plugins/index.html`.

 Tip   If you're looking for a browser-neutral source of downloadable plug-ins, check out CNET at `http://home.cnet.com/software/0-3227886-8-5419578-1.html`.

Table 12.1   HTML Tags Used in This Lesson

HTML Tag	Closing	Description of Use
`<embed>`	`</embed>`	Netscape's nonstandard, although largely supported, tag for including sound and video clips.
`<noembed>`	`</noembed>`	Netscape's tag that provides an alternate method of downloading the clip for browsers that don't recognize the `<embed>` tag.
`<object>`	`</object>`	W3C's preferred, although largely *un*supported, tag for including sound and video clips.

In this lesson, you've learned:

- Sound and video clips can be added to your Web page with the `<a>` tag.

- Both the `<object>` and the `<embed>` tags enable you to add a video clip with the video controls (start, stop, and so on) to your documents.

LESSON 13
Designing with HTML

In this lesson, you will learn some designer tricks of the trade to make your pages look as good as they work.

Design Basics

Web design may have had its roots in traditional paper design, but online design is different. One of the biggest differences when designing for online is the capability to *hyperlink*. Adding hyperlinks in your Web pages gives you the capability to quickly direct your viewers to the information you want them to see, including reference material on, or off, your Web site. Unfortunately, the capability to link also is one of the biggest disadvantages to online design. Occasionally, viewers get so caught up in clicking on all those "for additional information click here" links that they forget what they were looking for in the first place; in effect, they get lost in cyberspace.

To help their users recognize which Web pages are part of the same Web site, Web site designers have a number of design elements available to them to help set the mood for their Web site. The layout, images, navigation buttons, bullets, lines, colors, and even the fonts you choose should support the overall design theme of your site. In the following sections, you'll learn how each of these elements work together.

To design an effective Web page, you'll need to be aware of the differences in moving from traditional design to online design. Table 13.1 summarizes some of the differences. Knowing the problems you'll face is only half the battle; the rest is knowing how to avoid them. You'll learn that in the sections that follow.

Table 13.1   Paper Design Versus Online Design

Paper Design	Online Design
Viewers follow content along a linear path with a beginning, middle, and an end.	Using search tools or hyperlinks viewers can access the content at any point. The only way for you to control that movement is to provide hyperlinks and navigation.
Viewers can see an entire page (text and graphics) at the same time.	With larger graphics (or non-graphical browsers), viewers often have time to read the entire text before they ever see any images.
Serif fonts (such as Times Roman) usually are used for content; sans-serif fonts (such as Arial) usually are used for headings.	Sans-serif fonts usually are used for content; serif fonts usually are used for headings.
Viewers see an entire page (or multiple pages in a book or magazine layout). The size of the page, and the amount of content presented on it, is controlled by you, the author.	Viewers see only the amount of content that will fit on their monitor at one time, which often is only a couple of paragraphs of text. The viewer controls the presentation of the content with the size of their monitor and the browser settings.

Two whole fields of study, Information Design and Usability, are devoted to finding the most effective methods of communicating your message. Researchers in these fields have come up with some standard design guidelines that can help you make the most of the material you have to present. Following are some facts I'll bet you didn't know:

- Red, yellow, and green are the most difficult colors of text to read online. It's best not to use them or to use them sparingly. You'll learn more about colors and fonts in the subsequent sections.

- Your visitors read almost 50 percent slower online than on paper. You can counteract that by keeping your page length short (no more than two to three screen lengths) and providing tables and bulleted lists to give their eyes a rest from large blocks of text.

- Animated images and moving text catch the eye of potential visitors, but most people find them annoying if they continue to move while the visitor is trying to read or search for content on the page. You'll learn about these features in Lesson 15, "Creating Active Web Pages."

- If your visitors are looking for a particular piece of information, they will search your site for less than a minute before moving on to some other site, unless they are confident that you have the information they are looking for. A well-designed Web site will help your visitors find their information quickly. You'll learn how to do this in the "Layout, Content, and Navigation" section.

Layout, Content, and Navigation

Because people tend to read online text more slowly than paper text, Web site designers use *page layout* techniques to help make content more readable.

> **Page Layout**   The arrangement of text, graphics, and *whitespace* on a page.

> **Whitespace**   Refers to the background of a page. Note that this space does not have to be white.

In general, when designing a Web site, you will need to keep the following key tips in mind. Figure 13.1 shows you how some of these layout tricks work to emphasize your content.

- *Keep paragraphs short and include a margin*   Keep your paragraphs under ten lines and include a margin. If you want viewers to read your text, you'll need to make it easy for them. You learned how to use style sheets to create margins in Lesson 5, "Adding Your Own Style."

- *Break up long sections of text with bullets, tables, and headings* Information design research has shown that online readers scan text, rather than read it, until they find what they're looking for. Bullets and headings help users find things more quickly.

- *Don't underline any text unless it is a hyperlink*   Online viewers expect anything underlined to be clickable. If you use underlining for another purpose, such as formatting your headings, you will confuse your readers.

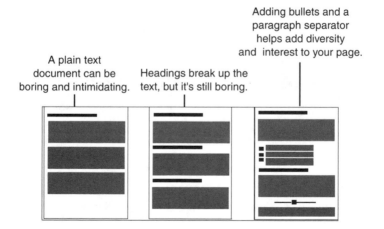

FIGURE 13.1   Adding diversity to your page layout helps enhance its readability.

If your Web site contains more than one page, you'll want to include some way for your visitors to find the other pages in your site. A good navigation system is more than a table of contents; it is a defined structure that gives your visitors information about your site. Your navigation system can consist of text links or image links (refer to Chapter 8, "Adding Images"). Whichever link type you choose, your navigation system should appear on every page of your site to help orient your users.

 Tip   Many designers use *frames* as a navigation tool. A frame is a portion of your HTML document that displays a separate HTML. You learned how to create frames, and use them effectively, in Lesson 10, "Creating Frames."

Fonts and Colors

Color is an exciting way to add interest to your Web pages. In addition to the obvious splash of color that images provide, you can add color to your fonts and page backgrounds. Be creative in your choices, but use a critical eye to review the results. Some colors are very difficult to read online and some color combinations are nearly impossible to decipher. Always provide some contrast in your color choice: use a light-colored font on a dark background and a dark-colored font on a light background.

 Tip   In HTML, colors are defined by name (such as navy, red, and black), or by a hexadecimal number. The six-digit number represents the amount of RGB (red, green, and blue) in the color. To see a list of colors and their numerical equivalent, check out these Web sites: http://the-light.com/colclick.html or http://www.hidaho.com/colorcenter/cc.html.

So, how do you add color? With style sheet properties, of course. HTML does have a <font> tag that enables you to specify a font (such as Arial or

Times Roman) and colors and sizes, but according to the W3C, users are not supposed to use it. Instead, they've given you the font-family, font-size, color, and background properties for your style sheets. The following code provides an example of how you can specify your fonts for the `<body>` and `<h1>` tags.

 Caution Just because you can specify a font doesn't mean that your visitor will have that font on his or her computer. To be on the safe side, always specify at least one alternate font, as I did in the following example. All but the most basic computers will have Arial and Times New Roman, so it's not a bad idea to use one of those two as your alternate font.

```
<!DOCTYPE html
     PUBLIC "-//W3C//DTD XHTML 1.0 Transitional//EN"
     "DTD/xhtml1-transitional.dtd">
<html xmlns="http://www.w3.org/1999/xhtml"
     xml:lang="en" lang="en">

<head>
<title>Fonts and Colors</title>
<style type="text/css">
body {font-family:Trebuchet MS, Arial;
     color:navy;
     font-size:12;
     background:white}
h1   {font-family:Bookman Old Style, Times New Roman;
     color:white;
     font-size:14;
     background:navy}
</style>
</head>
<body>
<h1>Fonts and Colors</h1>
<p>This text is navy on a white background, but the heading
   above is white on a navy background.</p>
</body>
</html>
```

By changing the values in the style properties, you change the results you see in the browser. Look at Figure 13.2 to see how the following changes affect what you see. By not adding a separate font-color and background property to the <h1> tag, the properties assigned in the <body> tag continue.

```
<style type="text/css">
body {font-family:Trebuchet MS;
      color:black;
      font-size:12;
      background:FFFF80}
h1    {font-family:Bookman Old Style;
      font-size:14}
</style>
```

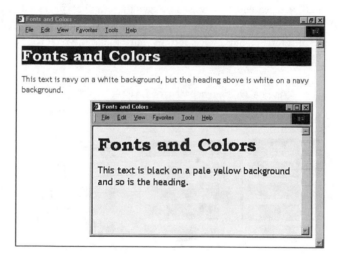

FIGURE **13.2**   The background property sets the background color of the entire tag, so using the property on the <body> tag sets the color for the entire page.

Tip   Don't get carried away with your font selections. A good rule of thumb is to use no more than three different fonts on each page: one font for the headings, one for the body text, and one for any special text, such as captions and pull-quotes.

Images

Like the other design elements discussed in this chapter, you should use images sparingly when they support the theme you've already established. In Lesson 8, you learned how to add images to your Web pages and use HTML and style sheet properties to align them with your text. Figure 13.3 shows the difference that balance and diversity make to your overall Web page layout.

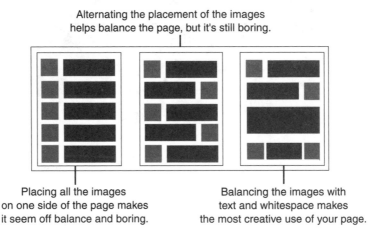

Alternating the placement of the images helps balance the page, but it's still boring.

Placing all the images on one side of the page makes it seem off balance and boring.

Balancing the images with text and whitespace makes the most creative use of your page.

Figure 13.3   Adding diversity to your graphical layout helps add interest.

Caution   Whenever you are working with graphics on a Web page, you need to be mindful of the overall size of the page. Most people will visit your Web site using a slow modem connection and might not be willing to wait for your page to finish loading. When you open your page using a modem, it should take no longer than five seconds to load. If your pages take much longer to load, you might try to reduce the image size, add thumbnails, or include some type of warning as to the fact that the page will take longer to load.

Background Images

Earlier, you learned how to add background color to your pages, but sometimes you'll want to add an image to the background of your page. The most prolific example of a background image is the page border (see Figure 13.4).

FIGURE 13.4   Use the background-image and margin style sheet properties to create a colored border on your Web page.

Here's how the source code looks for that page:

```
<!DOCTYPE html
       PUBLIC "-//W3C//DTD XHTML 1.0 Transitional//EN"
       "DTD/xhtml1-transitional.dtd">
<html xmlns="http://www.w3.org/1999/xhtml"
       xml:lang="en" lang="en">
<head>
<title>Using a Background Image</title>
<style type="text/css">
body {font-family:Trebuchet MS, Arial;
       color:black;
       font-size:14;
       background-image:url(images\background.gif);
       background-position:left top;
       margin:0,160}
h1     {font-family:Bookman Old Style, Times New Roman;
       color:A00068;
       font-size:18;
       background:white}
</style>
</head>
<body>
<h1>Background Images can be Fun</h1>
<p>I had to add a margin around this text or it would have
    begun inside the colored border area and defeated
    the purpose.</p>
</body>
</html>
```

The background.gif image is the colored border background. It is a GIF
file, which makes it small (only 5k) so that it will load quickly. I made it
in Paint Shop Pro by drawing a rectangle down the side of the page, as
shown in Figure 13.5.

You've already seen how you can use style sheet properties to set the
fonts and colors of the page, but look at the HTML source code for Figure
13.4 again to see that we've added three new style sheet properties for you
to learn:

- Background-image:url *(URL of file)*   The property tells the
  browser where to find the background image you want to use on
  your page. It must be used as part of the body style.

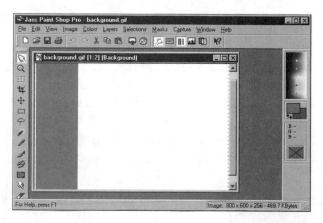

FIGURE **13.5**   The background.gif file was created in Paint Shop Pro.

- Background-position   This property tells the browser where to place the background image. This is assumed to be the top left (or left top), but you can specify any combination of the following vertical values: top, bottom, or center, and these horizontal values: left, right, or center.

- Margin   You can specify the margin property in inches (in), centimeters (cm), ems (em), points (pt), or pixels (px). If no unit of measure is specified, then the pixel unit is assumed. You can set the top, right, bottom, and left margins. I only set two of the margins for my background (0, 160). The browser knows that I wanted top=0px, right=160px, bottom=0px, and left=160px. The browser copied the first two values and applied the same values to the last two options. If I had only entered one value, the browser would have applied the same value to all four options.

If I hadn't set the margin property, the text on my page would have overlapped my image, as shown in Figure 13.6. The browser's even smart enough to add a white background to the heading text that overlaps the border.

> **Tip**   Don't forget to check out Lesson 5 if you want to know more about HTML style sheets.

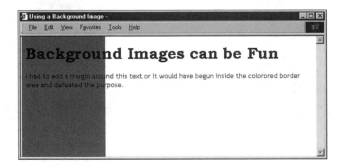

FIGURE **13.6**   Without the margin property, text starts at the left edge of the page.

In this lesson, you've learned:

- The layout, images, navigation buttons, bullets, lines, colors, and even the fonts that you choose should support the overall design theme of your site.

- Create interest in your Web pages by alternating the alignment of text and images, and by adding bulleted lists and tables.

- Just because you can specify a font doesn't mean that your visitor will have that font on his or her computer. To be on the safe side, always use Arial or Times New Roman as your alternate font.

LESSON 14
Creating Active Web Pages

In this lesson, you will learn about some of the advanced scripting tools that can enhance your Web pages. You'll also find some resources to help you learn more.

What Are Active Web Pages?

Normal HTML pages—everything you've created so far—are considered to be *static*. The page you create is the page that your visitors see, and (assuming that the pages are created without browser-specific code) all your visitors see the same thing.

Web applications and scripts enable your pages to change dynamically. You can use these techniques to make items onscreen change in relation to actions, such as a mouse click, that your visitors make.

Don't be scared off by the word *application*. There is some programming knowledge that is required to implement these elements into your Web pages, but not much. Unfortunately, I can't teach you everything there is to know about programming, but I can tell you where to find additional information.

The most popular ways of including active elements in your Web pages are described in the sections that follow. Table 14.1 gives a quick overview of the information in this lesson.

Table 14.1 Scripting and Programming

Technique	Browser	Comments
ActiveX	Microsoft Internet Explorer	ActiveX works on Netscape with a plug-in.
DHTML	All	Microsoft and Netscape disagree on how to implement DHTML. You might end up creating two sets of code to make everyone happy.
Java	All	Platform independent and can be used to create complex applications.
JavaScript	All	The best of everything. Works on all the major browsers, can be called from a plain HTML page, and you can find plenty of examples to copy into your own Web pages.
VBScript	Microsoft Internet Explorer	Easy to learn, but works on Internet Explorer only.

Java and ActiveX

Java and ActiveX are used to create Web applications. Java (created by Sun Microsystems) is platform independent (meaning that PCs, Macs, and UNIX systems can interpret the commands in the application). ActiveX (created by Microsoft), however, only works with the Internet Explorer browser. It is nearly impossible to guarantee that your visitors will use this browser unless you employ the annoying tactic that so many developers have chosen: preceding any application with a note warning your

visitors that they must download the *correct* browser before they can view
your pages.

How Do They Work?

Both Java and ActiveX work under the principle of object-oriented programming. The idea is that each piece of code should be treated as a separate entity, which can be used repeatedly in many types of environments,
including the Web.

Both elements can be embedded in your Web pages using HTML's
<object> tag. An <object>, in HTML, can be an image, an application,
or another HTML document. The attributes are the important distinction.
The first example (which follows) would be used to include a Java applet.
The second example would be used to include an ActiveX control (or
application).

```
<object codetype="application/java-archive"
        codebase="http://www.myWeb.com/apps/"
        classid="java:my.program.start">
</object>

<object codebase="http://www.myWeb.com/apps/"
        data="my.activex.program">
        classid="CLSID:613C8CCE-1FF8-41CF-A3DB-052336C14002">
</object>
```

In the first example, the classid attribute is the name of the Java applet
being called by the <object> tag. This same information appears in the
data attribute for ActiveX programs. In both examples, the codebase
attribute indicates the directory in which the application can be found.
However, the codebase attribute itself is not necessary. The entire URL
(including the base directory information) could be included in the
classid (for Java) and data (for ActiveX) attributes rather than including
the separate codebase attribute.

The ActiveX classid attribute deserves some explanation. Other than
telling you that the string of letters and numbers actually represents a
URL, the best help I can give is to inform you that any ActiveX control
that you choose to use in your Web page includes the appropriate classid
information so that you can copy it into your tag.

Tip   Find information about Java and download some fun Java applets at www.javasoft.com/applets/index.html.

You can find downloadable ActiveX controls at http://download.cnet.com/downloads/0-10081.html. You can find a plug-in to run these controls on Netscape at http://home.netscape.com/plugins/.

JavaScript and VBScript

Scripting is another type of programming, but it's easier to learn, which is a plus. Scripts can be added to an HTML document using the `<script>` tag. The tag can appear within the `<head>` or `<body>` of the document.

A script might be contained in a separate document that is called by the `<script>` tag (much as a linked style sheet is a separate document called by the `<style>` tag). A script might also be contained within the `<script>` tags in the HTML document itself. The decision is yours, based on how often you plan to use the script. If the script appears in only one page, incorporate the script into the document, as in the first of the following HTML samples. If the script appears on more than one page, make it a separate file so that you don't have to duplicate it, as in the second HTML sample.

```
<script type="text/vbscript">enter your script here.</script>
```

```
<script type="text/javascript"
        src="http://www.myweb.com/scripts/myscript.jss">
</script>
```

Although the `src` (source) attribute is only required when the script is contained in a separate file, the `type` attribute is always required. This attribute tells the browser which language the script is written in: `text/javascript`, `text/vbscript`, or `text/tcl`. If you are using the same scripting language throughout your HTML document, you can include a `<meta>` tag that defines the default script type for the entire document.

The `<meta>` tag (as you learned in Lesson 3, "Adding Text and More") is placed inside the `<head>` tag and gives the browser information about the document.

```
<meta http-equiv="Content-Script-Type" content="type">
```

What Can It Do?

The easy answer to this question is anything. If you look at some of the script collections on the Web, you find that people are using script for all kinds of things—including adding table values, creating rollover effects, and even games.

 Tip WebDeveloper has more than 7000 download-able JavaScript samples at `http://webdeveloper.earthweb.com/pagedev/webjs`.

MSDN's Online Code Center has even more code samples at `http://msdn.microsoft.com/code/`.

It is possible to associate a script with a certain event that occurs when the page appears on the browser. Figure 14.1 is an HTML page with some very simple JavaScript code that changes the background color of the page with the press of a button.

You might wonder where the code is because the `<script>` tag is empty. The code, in this case, is embedded in the `<input>` tag with the `onclick` command. The tag responds to each of the events shown in Table 14.2 and a few more.

Table 14.2 Script Calls

Event	With Tags	The Script Runs When...
onload	`<body>`, `<frameset>`	The document opens.
onunload	`<body>`, `<frameset>`	The document closes.

Table 14.2 Continued

Event	With Tags	The Script Runs When…
`onclick`	anything	The mouse is clicked over a particular item (button, image, and so on).
`ondblclick`	anything	The mouse is double-clicked over a particular item.
`onmouseover`	anything	The mouse is moved onto an item.
`onmouseout`	anything	The mouse moves away from an item.
`onmousemove`	anything	The mouse is moved while on an item.
`onsubmit`	Submit button	The form is submitted.
`onreset`	Reset button	The form is reset.

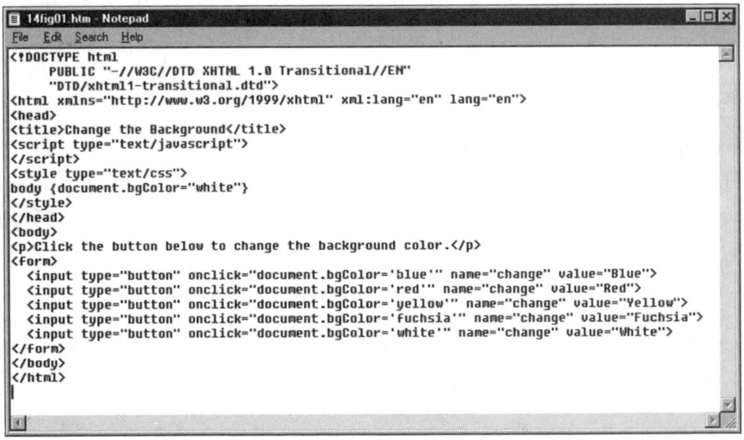


```
<!DOCTYPE html
     PUBLIC "-//W3C//DTD XHTML 1.0 Transitional//EN"
     "DTD/xhtml1-transitional.dtd">
<html xmlns="http://www.w3.org/1999/xhtml" xml:lang="en" lang="en">
<head>
<title>Change the Background</title>
<script type="text/javascript">
</script>
<style type="text/css">
body {document.bgColor="white"}
</style>
</head>
<body>
<p>Click the button below to change the background color.</p>
<form>
  <input type="button" onclick="document.bgColor='blue'" name="change" value="Blue">
  <input type="button" onclick="document.bgColor='red'" name="change" value="Red">
  <input type="button" onclick="document.bgColor='yellow'" name="change" value="Yellow">
  <input type="button" onclick="document.bgColor='fuchsia'" name="change" value="Fuchsia">
  <input type="button" onclick="document.bgColor='white'" name="change" value="White">
</form>
</body>
</html>
```

FIGURE 14.1 Simple JavaScript code to change the background color with the `onclick` command.

Tip   The event handlers (script calls) that tags support differ between browsers. Netscape supports many fewer event handlers than Internet Explorer does. Use ZDNET's compatibility table (http://www.zdnet.com/devhead/resources/tag_library/misc/event.html) to choose the right handler for your pages.

DHTML

DHTML is an acronym for *Dynamic HTML*. DHTML combines all the elements you've already learned (HTML, style sheets, and scripting) to create Web pages that are interactive and easy to update. Unfortunately, Microsoft, Netscape, and the World Wide Web Consortium (W3C) all disagree on how to accomplish this feat. The W3C doesn't even list the acronym on their Web site when discussing HTML standards.

Tip   See what Microsoft has to say about DHTML at http://msdn.microsoft.com/workshop/author/dhtml/dhtml.asp?frame=true.

You can find Netscape's description at http://developer.netscape.com/tech/dynhtml/.

Microsoft and Netscape do agree that DHTML should enable you to alter the appearance of a Web page after it has been loaded in the browser. They also agree that DHTML should enable developers to position any HTML element on a page. The elements can even be positioned in the same location so that, in effect, the elements appear on top of each other, but that's where the agreement ends.

Microsoft and Netscape have each developed their own browser-specific codes to achieve this type of interactivity. Using Microsoft's coding standards means that Netscape viewers might not be able to see the dynamic elements. The same is true if you use Netscape's coding standards. This diversity has meant that developers are forced to choose either to ignore a whole subset of their users, or to double-code all their pages to ensure that doesn't happen.

One of my favorite examples of a dynamic Web page is the MetLife Web site (www.metlife.com/). The center of the page changes depending on where I place my mouse. As Figure 14.2 shows, when I highlight the Company Info button, the center of the page tells me what type of content I'll see in that area of the Web site. When I move my mouse to another button, the center of the page changes again.

FIGURE 14.2   This Web site uses style sheets, absolute positioning, and JavaScript to dynamically alter the page.

The scope of this book does not allow for coverage of all these topics in any depth, but I hope you have some idea of the possibilities and can take the time to learn more on your own. Table 14.3 lists the HTML tags that were discussed in this lesson.

Table 14.3   HTML Tags Used in This Lesson

HTML Tag	Closing	Description of Use
<object>	</object>	Embeds an object, such as an application, into a Web page.
<script>	</script>	Embeds a script into a Web page.

In this lesson, you've learned:

- How to add Java and ActiveX applications to your HTML documents with the <object> tag.

- How to add JavaScript and VBScript to your HTML documents with the <script> tag.

- That DHTML combines all HTML, style sheets, and scripting to create Web pages that are interactive and easy to update.

LESSON 15
Web Page Authoring Tools

In this lesson, you will learn where to find some of the most popular Web page authoring tools and how you can use them to create your Web site.

Why Use a Tool?

You've just spent the last 14 lessons learning how to create Web pages by yourself, so why would you want to use a tool? The biggest reasons are time and ease of use. The Web is a very visual medium and staring at HTML code in a text editor is not very visually stimulating. It's easy to forget to be creative when you are concentrating so hard on making sure that you're using the correct HTML tags and putting them in the proper place in the document.

Web page authoring tools come with enough bells and whistles to get your Web site started in no time, and feature excellent site management and reporting tools. There are differences, though. FrontPage, for example, comes with a set of design themes that you can apply to your own pages to give your site a professional look. Dreamweaver has extensive support for style sheets. You can easily create style sheet declarations and apply them to the other pages in your Web site.

FrontPage and Dreamweaver are consistently voted best of the best and you might find that they help you, too. In the following sections, I want to introduce you to some of the most interesting features of both products.

Microsoft FrontPage

FrontPage contains a little bit of everything. It has site management fea-tures, predesigned Web themes, starter Webs that are ready for your con-tent, and advanced features (such as navigation buttons and search bots); all with a familiar interface that feels like a combination of Microsoft Word and the Windows Explorer. Figure 15.1 shows a sample page in FrontPage.

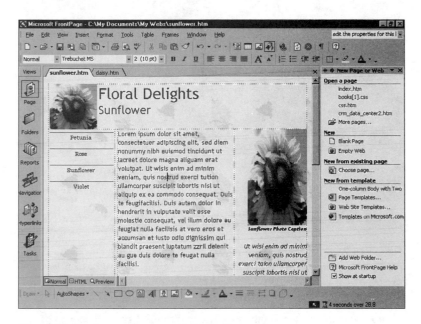

FIGURE 15.1   A sample page in FrontPage.

One of the best features FrontPage has going for it, aside from the fact that the interface is so familiar to most computer users, is that it includes a variety of Web wizards that you can use to define the type of site and the type of pages you want to have. Select a design theme and the program creates all your pages and adds Navigation bars with the hyperlinks already in place. You just add the basic content in the middle of the page.

The Navigation view of FrontPage is exciting as well. You can add, remove, or rearrange the pages in your Web site and FrontPage automatically updates the Navigation bar. (See Figure 15.2.)

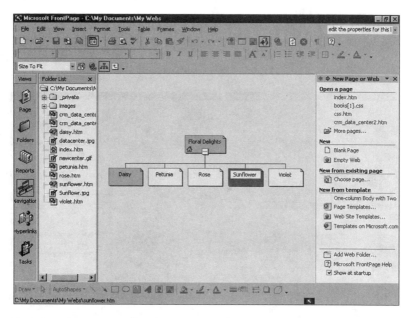

FIGURE 15.2   The Navigation view in FrontPage. You can add, remove, or rearrange pages in this view and the Navigation bar is automatically updated.

FrontPage is available with the Professional Special Edition version of Office; it can also be purchased separately. It integrates well with the other Microsoft Office software packages, such as Word, Excel, and Access. You can even create a Web page in Microsoft Word, save it as a Web page in your FrontPage Web site, and apply the FrontPage Web theme to the finished product without losing your original formatting.

FrontPage supports basic database interactivity well. It can create and update an Access database from a form. In addition, extensive toolbars, menu choices, and shortcut menus make it easy to add your content without cluttering up the editing window. The tabs at the bottom of the

FrontPage window enable you to see the actual HTML source code for your page. (See Figure 15.3.)

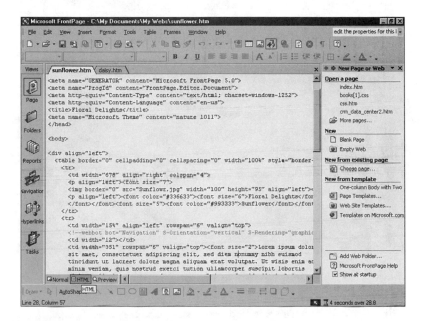

FIGURE **15.3**   The HTML Source view of FrontPage.

FrontPage has another feature that you might enjoy using on your Web sites. It includes the ability to add content from some of Microsoft's most popular Web sites (such as Expedia, MSNBC, and bCentral). In Figure 15.4, for instance, you can see that the MSNBC component includes headlines from the News, Living and Travel, Business, and three other sections.

> **Tip**   You can find out more about FrontPage at Microsoft's FrontPage Web site (www.microsoft.com/frontpage/default.htm).

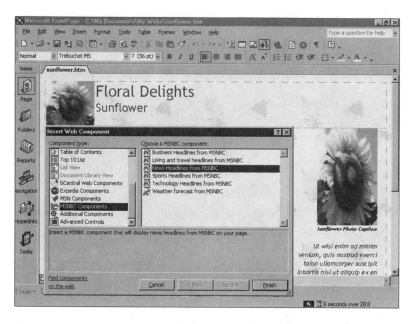

FIGURE 15.4   Inserting a FrontPage Web Component.

FrontPage does provide some fairly advanced page components that include an ad banner manager, a hit counter, a search bot, hover buttons, and scheduled image and page substitutions. Most of these features, however, require FrontPage server extensions that you can download free from Microsoft's site.

Caution   Be aware that if you create a Web site in FrontPage and want to publish it to the World Wide Web, you need to find a Web host that supports these server extensions.

Macromedia Dreamweaver

Dreamweaver does not come packaged with any templates, themes, or wizards to help you get started; nor does it feature a "looks like Microsoft

Word" interface. (See Figure 15.5.) In fact, the interface takes some getting used to because there are floating toolbars everywhere, but those same toolbars offer a variety of ways to enhance the pages that you create. (See Figure 15.6.)

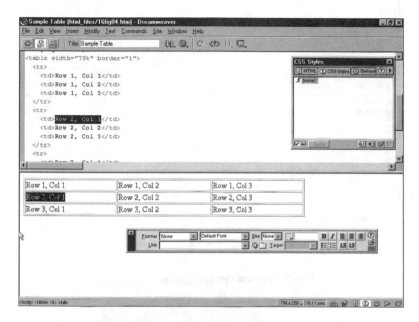

FIGURE **15.5**   A sample page in Dreamweaver.

After you design a page, you can create a template with editable and noneditable regions, which you then can use to build other pages on your site. What's more, if you change your template somewhere down the line, Dreamweaver automatically updates any page created with the template. You can use Dreamweaver's Styles window to create style sheet declarations by example and store those styles for recall in other pages. (See Figure 15.7.)

The Site window enables you to manage your site's content. You can also upload files into your site. Dreamweaver does not retain the formatting of imported word processor files, but it does an excellent job of incorporating HTML files. Unlike FrontPage, however, Dreamweaver doesn't automatically create Navigation bars.

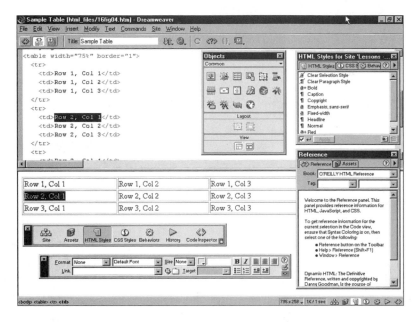

FIGURE 15.6   The same page with floating toolbars exposed.

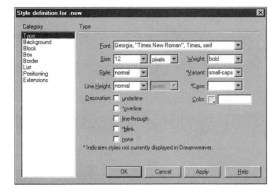

FIGURE 15.7   Style sheets are easily created and modified.

One of my favorite features is Dreamweaver's Objects palette, shown in Figure 15.8. A pop-up menu enables you to switch between the four panels described in the following list. These panels enable you to easily insert objects in your pages.

- The Common panel contains the most commonly used objects (such as images, tables, horizontal lines, layers, and multimedia objects).

- The Forms panel contains buttons for creating forms and inserting form fields.

- The Head panel contains objects for adding various <head> elements (such as the <meta> and <title> tags).

- The Special panel contains objects for adding Java applets, ActiveX components, and plug-ins.

- The Invisibles panel contains buttons for creating objects that are not visible in the Document window (such as named anchors <a name="*name*"> and comments).

FIGURE **15.8**   The Objects palette makes inserting frequently used elements easy.

Dreamweaver excels at the advanced features, such as layering and XML compliance. Even though most browsers can't agree on how to support these features, Dreamweaver can check your page for compatibility with several versions of both Internet Explorer and Netscape Navigator, and verify all your internal links.

Unlike FrontPage, Dreamweaver doesn't require special server extensions or add extraneous code to your pages, which means that you are able to use your pages with any Web host.

Other Popular Web Tools

FrontPage and Dreamweaver aren't the only Web authoring tools available. Several more appear in the following list, along with a link to a product review from PC Computing:

- *Adobe GoLive* `http://www.zdnet.com/products/stories/`
  `reviews/0,4161,2638081,00.html`

- *HoTMetaL PRO* `http://www.zdnet.com/products/stories/`
  `reviews/0,4161,2771504,00.html`

- *NetObjects Fusion MX*
  `http://www.zdnet.com/products/stories/`
  `reviews/0,4161,2771530,00.html`

- *BBEdit* `http://www.hallogram.com/barebones/?source=goto`

If you don't like the idea of a WYSIWYG tool and you prefer to continue working directly with the HTML source code, you probably will like HomeSite. With HomeSite, you can drag and drop HTML code, insert links, and modify existing tags. You can also search and replace HTML code, and when you're confused about which attributes apply to which tags, HomeSite can offer suggestions. All this makes HomeSite the choice of many professional developers. You can read more about HomeSite at `http://www.allaire.com/Products/HomeSite/overview.cfm`.

In this lesson, you've learned:

- Microsoft FrontPage is perfect for beginners. It looks like Microsoft Word and comes with many preformatted designs.

- Macromedia's Dreamweaver has advanced features, such as style sheet controls and layering, that make it perfect for professionals.

- Both tools enable you to create Web pages without knowing the HTML tags that you're learning in this book.

Lesson 16

Making a Name for Yourself

In this lesson, you will learn where to find a Web host to publish your Web site and tips for making sure your site is found.

Web Hosting

When you finally finish creating your Web pages, you're going to want to put them on the Internet and make sure they're found. Unless you plan to set up your own Web server, you'll probably be looking for a *Web hosting* service.

> **Web Host** A company that provides space on its Web servers to store your Web files.

Web hosting services offer help in a variety of ways, and at a variety of costs. Some Web hosts offer design services, customizable scripts, visitor logs, database support, and more (in addition to the standard disk space). Use the information in Table 16.1 to find a Web host that meets your needs.

Table 16.1   Web Hosting Resources

Host Name	Comments	URL
The List	The official list of Internet Service Providers	`thelist.internet.com`
Web Host Power Search	Find a Web host by selecting from a feature list	`webservices.cnet.com/cgi/scompare.asp?stable=Hosting_Plans`
Yahoo! Geocities	Free Web hosting with authoring resources	`geocities.yahoo.com/home/`
Tripod	Free Web hosting	`www.tripod.com`
Cybercities	Free Web hosting	`www.cybercities.com`
Register FrontPage Hosts	Web hosts that support Microsoft FrontPage, and who have registered with Microsoft	`www.microsoftwpp.com/default.asp`

Search Pages and Indexes

After your HTML documents are up and running on a Web server, you need to make sure that people can find them. Because most people look to *search engines* when they want to find something on the Internet, we'll start there.

Search Engines   Searchable indexes of Web resources. Some search engines (called *indexes*) also categorize information enabling people to search by categories and keywords.

Two types of search engines exist on the Web: spiders and indexes.

- A *spider* (also called a Web crawler, or *bot*, which is short for robot) is an automated script that crawls through Web pages following hyperlinks to find related pages, and then builds a database with the contents of all the pages it visits.

- A *search index* is an automated script that looks in a prepopulated database for pages containing specific words or phrases. The search index's administrative personnel review the content of the pages and populate the database.

Search Bots

Search engine bots (also called robots, spiders, and crawlers) search through all Web pages and then index them according to the information they find. You can help the indexing portion be more accurate by using <meta> tags. Without <meta> tags, these bots treat every word in a document exactly alike. If you add keywords and descriptions to your documents, you increase the possibility that your Web pages will be found. You learned how to do this in Lesson 3, "Adding Text and More," but let's try a quick refresher. The following example shows the correct format for adding the <meta> tag to your documents. Figure 16.1 is an actual example of the <meta> tags used on the WebReference.com site.

```
<!DOCTYPE html
     PUBLIC "-//W3C//DTD XHTML 1.0 Transitional//EN"
     "DTD/xhtml1-transitional.dtd">
<html xmlns="http://www.w3.org/1999/xhtml"
     xml:lang="en" lang="en">
<head>
<title>Your HTML Page</title>
<meta name="keywords" contents="keywords that
          people might use to search
          for your page.">
<meta name="description" contents="a brief
          paragraph describing your
          document.">
<meta name="author" contents="your name">
</head>
<style type="text/css">
```

```
</style>
<body>
    insert your document here.
</body>
</html>
```

```
dhtml[1] - Notepad                                                    _ 8 X
File  Edit  Search  Help
<HTML>
<HEAD><TITLE>DHTML Lab: Dynamic HTML Tutorials, DHTML Scripts, Programming,
Tools, Code, and Examples - dhtmlab.com</TITLE>
<META NAME="keywords" CONTENT="dhtml dynamic html tutorial javascript programming tool computer
software internet explorer java script communicator database animation jscript layers cascading
stylesheet design CSS webmaster browser authoring development vbscript designer table learning
dhtml hierarchal menu free example library demo editor sample code parser guru peter belesis
dynomat webreference.com dynamic headline fader cross browser dhtmlab.com jigsaw puzzle games
diner dhtml.com">
<META NAME="description" CONTENT="Dynamic HTML Lab offers biweekly dhtml tutorials and more.
Learn how to create low bandwidth animations, databases, presentations and more using style
sheets, layers, positioning, and JavaScript.">
<STYLE TYPE='text/css'>
<!--
A:hover{color:blue}
A.white{text-decoration:none;color:white}
TT{font-size:10pt;font-family:monospace;color:#009}
TD.menu{cursor:hand;background-color:#9C3063;color:white;font-weight:bold;font-family:Arial,sans-
serif;font-size:9pt;text-align:right}
.sans{font-family:Arial,Verdana,sans-serif;font-size:10pt}
.sansb{font-family:Arial,Verdana,sans-serif;font-size:10pt;font-weight:bold}
.browsers{display:inline;font-family:sans-serif;font-size:9pt;font-weight:bold}
.latest{border:1px black solid; padding:5;font-family:Arial,Verdana,sans-serif;font-size:10pt}
H3.regular{color:black;font-size:100%;font-family:Times;font-weight:bold}
A.columns{text-decoration:underline;font-family:sans-serif;font-size:10pt;font-weight:bold}
UL,LI{font-family:Arial,Verdana,sans-serif;font-size:10pt}
.s {margin-bottom:4px;}
.news {color:#660099;font-size:10pt;line-height:12pt;}
-->
</STYLE>
<STYLE TYPE="text/css">
<!--
FORM.tb {display:inline;}
  .twidth{width:100%}
    .include{ font-size: 75%; font-family: verdana, arial, helvetica;}
    .includebig{font-family: verdana, arial, helvetica;}
    .includebig A:link { color: blue; }
```

FIGURE 16.1   The HTML source code for `http://webreference.`
`com/dhtml/` with the `<meta>` tags highlighted.

Tip   If you don't add any other `<meta>` tags, be sure
to add the description. Not all search engines rank
pages in the same manner, but they all display a
description of the pages found. The right description
can lure visitors to your site.

Adding Your Web Site to the Search Engine

All search engines enable Web authors to add the URL of their own Web site to the search engine. Most of them do this with some type of online form. A link to Yahoo!'s Suggest a Site form (`http://docs.yahoo.com/info/suggest/`) appears at the bottom of every Yahoo! Page. (See Figures 16.2 and 16.3.) Yahoo! requires you to find the appropriate category for your Web page before submitting the site. In this way, Yahoo! adds the category information to the rest of your information to help rank your pages.

The Submit a Site form (`http://www.excite.com/info/add_url`) on Excite's search engine page asks only for the URL of your home page and some contact information. (See Figure 16.4.) Other search engines require similar information before adding your site to their list.

Tip   Some Web sites offer to add your URL to many (if not all) search sites with one form. Companies such as `www.submit-it.com`, for instance, charge a fee for this convenience. However, you probably want to add your own site information to the most popular search sites (Yahoo!, Excite, AltaVista, Lycos, LookSmart, and Go.com) to assure yourself the best chance of being found.

FIGURE 16.2   Yahoo!'s Suggest a Site page enables you to add your Web page to the Yahoo! index.

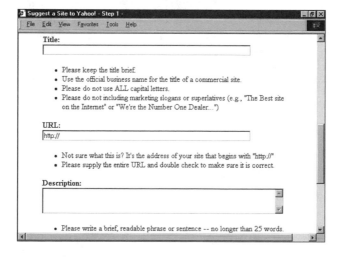

FIGURE 16.3   Yahoo!'s Suggest a Site form enables you to control the description that Yahoo! displays for your Web site.

FIGURE 16.4   Excite's Submit a Site form.

Advertising

Don't forget that you can advertise on the Web, too. The following list of
Web sites offers some form of advertising or announcement service. The
flashy banner ads that proliferate the Web are there for a reason: People
actually click on them. These advertising services can help you create
your own ad and place it on pages that relate to your site.

- http://dir.yahoo.com/Computers_and_Internet/Internet/
  World_Wide_Web/Site_Announcement_and_Promotion/

- www.smartage.com/excite_clicks/

- www.banneradnetwork.com

> **Tip**   Remember to include your URL on your business
> cards, letterhead, and e-mail auto-signature. Unless
> you tell people where to look, they can't find you.

In this lesson, you've learned:

- Two types of search engines exist on the Web: spiders and indexes.

- To add keywords for the search engines with `<meta>` tags. Different search engines search for different `<meta>` tags, so use several (including keywords, descriptions, and author).

- Most search engines have their own site-submittal forms. Fill out these forms so that the search engine can find your site.

LESSON 17
XML and the Future of the Internet

In this lesson, you will learn what's next for the Internet and what you can do now to prepare for the coming changes.

The Future of the Internet

The extraordinary growth of the Internet since the early 1990s has come about chiefly because HTML is so easy to learn. Companies can distribute information to their employees, customers, and business partners quickly and inexpensively. Unfortunately (or fortunately, depending on your point of view), the first blush of Internet and Web development has passed and companies are already beginning to look for new ways to disseminate the information they want to share.

Hearing this cry for help, the World Wide Web Consortium has developed an eXtensible Markup Language (XML) that can be used by Web page authors whose needs extend beyond the capabilities of HTML.

> **eXtensible Markup Language (XML)** The newest language being developed by the World Wide Web Consortium, XML has been described as a language for defining other languages. It is more flexible than HTML.

What Is XML?

To understand XML, you need to step back and remember what HTML is. HTML is a markup language that uses a predefined set of tags to describe a document's structure in terms of paragraphs, headings, and so on. Like HTML, XML describes the structure of the document, but unlike HTML, XML is flexible enough (or *extensible* enough) to define the same tag name (such as `<title>`) in several different ways depending on which *Document Type Definition (DTD)* is called.

In addition, XML takes the concept of tagging one step further by enabling developers to create custom tags and attributes. Both markup languages use style sheets to define the format of each tag with color, fonts, and emphasis.

> **Document Type Definition (DTD)**   A file defining the set of tags that can be used within a particular file. XHTML uses three DTDs: strict, transitional, and frameset.

The following examples show how a single entry from an address book might be marked up in both HTML and XML, respectively:

- HTML:

```
<p>The White House<br />
1600 Pennsylvania Avenue NW<br />
Washington, DC  20500</p>
```

- XML:

```
<contact>
  <name>The White House</name>
  <address>1600 Pennsylvania Avenue NW</address>
  <city>Washington</city>
  <state>DC</state>
  <zip>20500</zip>
</contact>
```

Why is this difference important? It's important because, in essence, your document becomes a giant database of information.

Suppose that I am the owner of a chain of multiplex theaters and I want to put information on the Web about the movies I'm showing. In traditional Web publishing (if something as young as the World Wide Web can be said to even have a traditional method), I could do one of the following two things:

- Create a series of Web pages that would need to be updated frequently.

- Create a database that held all the information and hire a Java programmer to write an application that would enable people to perform searches on my database to see what was showing in their neighborhood.

With the advent of XML, I have a third option. I can create a single Web page that contains all the information for all my theaters, and then use style sheets and templates to present the right information to the right people.

> **Tip**   The W3C and industry experts are creating industry-specific versions of the XML standard. So, you can create your own tags in XML, and you can also take advantage of the fact that others in your industry are using the same standard.

Analyze the Data

The first thing I have to do is analyze my data. What information do I need to share? I probably would want to share the name of the movie, a brief description, the names of the stars in the movie, links to promotional information for the film, the name of the theater in which it's playing, the address of the theater, my phone number, the time the movie is showing, the price of the ticket, whether discounts are available, and a lot more.

After you know the type of data you need to collect, you can create your XML input document. You can see an example of two of these input documents in Figure 17.1. Each data type is represented by a pair of tags (such as `<movies>` and `</movies>`). Related data types are nested within a parent tag. For example, the `<title>` and `<star-male>` tags are related to the `<movies>` tag. Unlike with HTML, I made up my own XML tags based on the information I wanted to present.

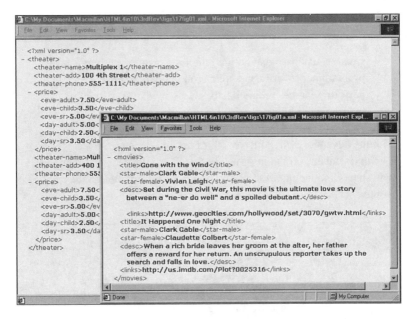

FIGURE **17.1**   Without a style sheet, an XML-enabled browser can only render text.

Caution Don't rush out to convert all your HTML documents to XML just yet. Most browsers can't process XML documents yet. However, you can start preparing now by creating XHTML documents. These documents enable you to use HTML and XHMTL now, and will be easy to convert to XML in the future.

Create a Style Sheet Template

After you complete the input document, you need to create a style sheet template that determines how you present your information. You learned about style sheets in Lesson 5, "Creating Your Own Style." XML style sheet templates are very similar, but also define the structure of the document (tables, lists, paragraphs, and so on).

 Tip   You can learn more about XML style sheet templates from the W3C at www.w3.org/TR/xsl/. Another excellent resource for XML information is www.xml.com.

The real fun with XML documents comes from the fact that the content of the page is separated from its format. In the movie theater example, suppose that I own two movie theaters. Multiplex 1 is a downtown art theater (refer to Figure 17.1). It only shows artsy films attended by serious film students and it likes to promote itself as a dark, almost somber, environment. Multiplex 2 is in a posh part of uptown and shows mostly revivals to an older, more conservative crowd. Now imagine that I'm planning to show the same movie, *Citizen Kane*, at both theaters.

My input document, which holds the content that appears on the Web site for both theaters, includes the following tags for *Citizen Kane*:

```
<title>Citizen Kane</title>
<star-male>Orson Wells</star-male>
<desc>Powerful newspaper owner Charles Foster Kane was many
        things to many people, both in life and, as seen in
        retrospective, in death.</desc>
<links>http://us.imdb.com/Plot?0033467</links>
```

Using XML style sheet templates, I can create two completely different pages for my theaters. For Multiplex 1, the artsy theater, I might choose to have a black background with the title in a dramatic gothic-looking font and the other elements (<star-male>, <desc>, and <links>) placed in a bulleted list below. For Multiplex 2, the revival theater, I might create a background image of a film canister for my page. Then, I might choose to place all the elements of the movie into a horizontal table for a more conservative feel.

I can do that because style sheet properties reference the element they are defining, not the content of that element. Rather than placing the content (*Citizen Kane*) on the style sheet template, I would place the following tag, which tells your computer to insert the information in the <title> tag.

```
<xsl:value-of select="title"/>
```

XML promises to be a platform-independent, software-independent language. Web developers and other programmers will be able to use the same data input documents to present information on the Web, in business automation tools (such as spreadsheets and word processors), and even on paper. That can save us all a lot of time and money.

Planning for the Future

More and more, computer application developers are choosing to create their applications using Web technology. Whereas just 10 years ago, schools were busy teaching their students how to write BASIC programs and type DOS commands at the appropriate prompts, now they are teaching students HTML and learning to browse the Internet is a requirement. Some schools even offer homework help on the Internet. The Internet and Web technology are not going away, and they are going to continue to grow and change.

Already we are seeing the emergence of cell phones, pagers, and other hand-held devices that can display some Internet sites. The release of the XML standard will enable the Internet to become available in any number of new media. That's why it is important to understand what you can do now to make sure that you aren't caught off guard the next time the standard changes.

Check Your Code

Microsoft and Netscape, the two largest competitors in the browser wars, continue to try and outdo each other with new browser features. Both browsers have been known to create new tags that work only on their own browser. If you use those tags when you are creating your Web site, you end up forcing your viewers to choose a browser, or lose important features that you intended to share with them. Don't put them in that position. You can use tools, such as Web Site Garage's TuneUp (http://websitegarage.netscape.com/O=wsg/tuneup_plus/index.html), to ensure that your site is the best it can be.

Be sure to test your pages on different browsers and older browser versions. Not everyone uses the newest version of a browser and some older versions do not support as many tags. The Browser Snapshot feature at the Web Site Garage does this for a small fee. Figure 17.2 shows what you can expect from their service. Above the browser screenshot, Web Site Garage tells you which browser (and at what resolution) the screenshot was taken.

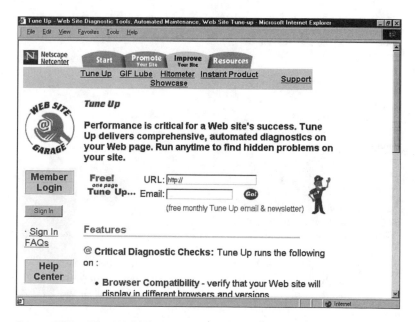

FIGURE **17.2**   The Web Site Garage can test your pages for browser compatibility.

Use Correct Syntax

XHMTL must be well-formed; in other words, tags must be nested properly (see the "Nest Tags Properly" section later in this lesson) and tags
must be closed. For example, if you forget to close your `<li>` (list item)
tag within a `<ul>` (unordered or bulleted list), the browser knows that
when you add the next `<li>` tag, you want the last one to close. In fact,
you want all of your tags to close. In HTML, the following:

```
<ul>
<li>One ring-y, ding-y</li>
<li>Two ring-y, ding-ys</li>
</ul>
```

is the same as this:

```
<ul>
<li>One ring-y, ding-y
<li>Two ring-y, ding-ys
</ul>
```

and the same as this:

```
<UL>
<LI>One ring-y, ding-y</LI>
<LI>Two ring-y, ding-ys</LI>
</UL>
```

and the same as this:

```
<ul>
<Li>One ring-y, ding-y</Li>
<LI>Two ring-y, ding-ys</li>
</Ul>
```

With XHTML documents, browsers can differentiate between those
examples. Only the first example is well-formed. Learn now to use the
proper syntax for your documents and you won't find yourself reworking
them later.

 Tip Did you notice in the examples that capitaliza-
tion of the tags makes a difference in XHTML? It's all
part of the syntax.

Always Quote Attributes

All tag attributes must be quoted. In the past, you could add attributes, as in the following HTML sample:

```
<img src=/images/trial/gavel.jpg />
```

However, the new XHTML standard (in an effort to prepare us for the transition to XML) requires us to enclose all the attribute specifications in quotes, as in the following HTML sample:

```
<img src="/images/trial/gavel.jpg" />
```

These are minor differences, sure, but if you get into the habit of doing this correctly from the start, it will save a tremendous amount of rework as the standard is fine-tuned.

Use Style Sheets

In previous versions of HTML, Web page authors controlled the color, format, and layout of their documents with formatting tags (such as `<font color="color" size="size" family="font name">` and `<body bgcolor="color">`). With XHTML, the W3C is recommending that all these format attributes be controlled with style sheets instead.

This book has focused on the XHTML preferences, which might mean that older browsers won't always show what you intend. You can add older HTML tags to your documents without affecting your style sheets, as shown in Figure 17.3. Just remember that the HTML format tags and the style sheet properties cannot conflict, or you will have problems. If your style sheet property tells the browser that the `<body>` tag should have a yellow background, for example, be sure that the `<body>` tag also calls for a yellow background. If you choose conflicting attributes by mistake (as is done in the following example where the style sheet requires the background color to be #FFFF80, but the `<body>` tag requires the background color to be white), the style sheet property takes precedence.

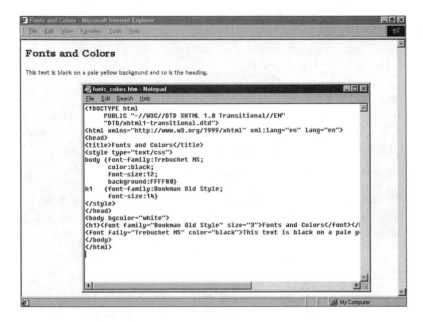

FIGURE 17.3   The HTML document seen in Figure 13.2 now has formatting tags added for older browsers.

Nest Tags Properly

Because XHTML and XML are more structured than HTML, you should get into the habit of paying attention to the details. You've seen in previous lessons that you can nest one HTML tag inside another. If you want to have text within a table cell (or any tagged element, such as a <ul>, <li>, and so on) to be both bold and italic, remember to close the tags in the order that you opened them. The following example shows that <b> was opened first and closed last.

```
<table>
<tr>
<td>
<b><i>This is bold and italicized text.</i></b>
</td>
</tr>
</table>
```

You might nest tags within a paragraph, as shown in the following example. The first two sentences are both bold, although only the second is italicized. Remember to add the second `<i>` tag. You'll be glad you did when HTML and the browsers require it.

```
<b>Bold<i>Bold and italicized</i></b><i>Italicized</i>
```

Check It Twice

It's such a simple thing that we often overlook it, but your pages appear more professional and your visitors have more respect for the information you provide, if your content is spelled correctly.

By the same token, don't publish broken links. Nothing is worse than clicking a link that goes nowhere, or leads to the dreaded 404 error. Make sure you verify that all your links go where you want them to go.

 Caution Whatever you do, don't forget to verify that your document includes the correct DTD: strict, transitional, or frameset. The document is not XHTML-compliant if it doesn't include the DTD.

Learn All You Can

The Internet is a great place to learn about HTML, XML, and the World Wide Web. Check out some of the following great resources:

- W3C's HTML and XHTML Specifications
  www.w3.org/MarkUp/

- W3C's XML 1.0 Recommendation
  www.w3.org/XML/

- XML, Java, and the Future of the Web
  http://www.ibiblio.org/pub/
  sun-info/standards/xml/why/xmlapps.htm

- XML Resource Center
  www.xml.com

- CNET's Spotlight on Advanced Technologies
  `http://builder.cnet.com/webbuilding/`
  `0-7267.html?tag=st.bl.3882.dir1.7267`

In this lesson, you've learned:

- XML goes beyond HTML. Rather than just assigning a structure to the text (with paragraphs, headings, tables, and so on), XML adds meaning and order.

- The XML standard isn't complete yet, but it will take over the Internet when it is.

- There are things you can do now to ensure that you are ready for the future of the Internet: use the correct syntax for all tags, use lowercase HTML tags, nest your tags appropriately, and use style sheets rather than the HTML formatting codes.

APPENDIX A

XHTML Quick Reference

XHTML is an ambitious attempt to meet the needs of Web developers worldwide, both casual and professional. XHTML is a reformulation of HTML as an XML application. It enables extensions to the language to be more easily defined and implemented. This appendix provides a quick reference to most of the elements and attributes defined by the HTML 4 specification for use in XHTML documents.

 Tip This appendix is based on the information provided in the *HTML 4.0 Specification W3C Recommendation* (revised on December 24, 1999), and on the *XHTML 1.0 Specification W3C Recommendation* (revised on January 26, 2000). The latest versions of these standards can be found at http://www.w3.org/.

To make the information readily accessible, this appendix organizes HTML elements by their function in the following order:

- Required Elements
- Text Phrases and Paragraphs
- Lists
- Links

- Tables

- Embedded Content

- Style

- Forms

- Scripts

The elements are listed alphabetically within each section, and the following information is presented:

- Usage   A general description of the element.

- Attributes   Lists the attributes of the element with a short description of their effect.

- Notes   Relates any special considerations when using the element.

> **Caution**   Several elements and attributes of HTML have been deprecated by the current XHTML specification. They have been outdated and you should avoid using them. Those deprecated elements and attributes have been eliminated in this appendix.

Following this, the common attributes and intrinsic events are summarized.

Required Elements

XHTML relies on several elements to define the document as well as to provide information that is used by the browser or search engine.

Tip   Several common attributes used for structure, internationalization, and events are abbreviated as core, i18n, and events in the following quick reference sections. The description for each of these abbreviations can be found later in the "Common Attributes and Events" section.

\<body>...\</body>

Usage	Contains the document's content.
Attributes	core, i18n, events.
	onload="..." Intrinsic event triggered when the document loads.
	onunload="..." Intrinsic event triggered when the document unloads.
Notes	There can be only one \<body>, and it must follow the \<head>. The \<body> element can be replaced by a \<frameset> element.

\<!DOCTYPE>

Usage	Version information appears on the first line of an HTML document and is an SGML declaration rather than an element.
Attributes	html PUBLIC "-//W3C//DTD XHTML 1.0 Strict//EN" "DTD/xhtml1-strict.dtd"> Used for documents following the strict XHTML requirements.

```
html PUBLIC "-//W3C//DTD XHTML 1.0
Transitional//EN" "DTD/xhtml1-
transitional.dtd">
```
Used for documents following the XHTML requirements, but also including some deprecated elements.

```
html PUBLIC "-//W3C//DTD XHTML 1.0
Frameset//EN" "DTD/xhtml1-frameset.dtd">
```
Used for framed documents.

<head>...</head>

Usage	This is the document header and contains other elements that provide information to users and search engines.
Attributes	i18n.
	profile="..." URL specifying the location of meta data.
Notes	Strict DTD. There can be only one <head> per document. It must follow the opening <html> tag and precede the <body>.

<html>...</html>

Usage	The html element contains the entire document.
Attributes	i18n.

`<meta />`

Usage	Provides information about the document.
Attributes	`i18n.`
	`http-equiv="..."` HTTP response header name.
	`name="..."` Name of the `meta` information.
	`content="..."` Content of the `meta` information.
	`scheme="..."` Assigns a scheme to interpret the `meta` data.

`<title>...</title>`

Usage	This is the name you give your Web page. The `<title>` element is located in the `<head>` element and is displayed in the browser window title bar.
Attributes	`i18n.`

Text Phrases and Paragraphs

Text phrases (or blocks) can be structured to suit a specific purpose, such as creating a paragraph. This should not be confused with modifying the formatting of the text.

`<address>...</address>`

Usage	Provides a special format for author or contact information.
Attributes	`core, i18n, events.`
Notes	The ` ` element is commonly used inside the `<address>` element to break the lines of an address.

`<blockquote>...</blockquote>`

Usage	Used to display long quotations.
Attributes	`core, i18n, events.`
	`cite="..."` The URL of the quoted text.

`<br />`

Usage	Forces a line break.
Attributes	`core, i18n, events.`
	`clear="..."` Sets the location where the next line begins after a floating object (`none, left, right, all`).

`<div>...</div>`

Usage	The division element is used to add structure to a block of text.
Attributes	`core, i18n, events.`
Notes	Cannot be used within a `<p>` element.

`<em>...</em>`

Usage	Emphasized text.
Attributes	`core, i18n, events.`

`<h1>...</h1>–<h6>...</h6>`

Usage	The six headings (`h1` is uppermost, or most important) are used in the `body` to structure information in a hierarchical fashion.

Attributes	`core, i18n, events`.
Notes	Visual browsers display the size of the headings in relation to their importance, `<h1>` being the largest and `<h6>` the smallest.

`<p>...</p>`

Usage	Defines a paragraph.
Attributes	`core, i18n, events`.

`<pre>...</pre>`

Usage	Displays preformatted text.
Attributes	`core, i18n, events`.
	`width="..."` The width of the formatted text.

`<strong>...</strong>`

Usage	Stronger emphasis.
Attributes	`core, i18n, events`.

`<sub>...</sub>`

Usage	Creates subscript.
Attributes	`core, i18n, events`.

`<sup>...</sup>`

Usage	Creates superscript.
Attributes	`core, i18n, events`.

Text Formatting Elements

Text characteristics such as the size, weight, and style can be modified using these elements, but the XHTML specification encourages you to use style sheets instead.

`<b>...</b>`

Usage	Bold text.
Attributes	core, i18n, events.

`<big>...</big>`

Usage	Large text.
Attributes	core, i18n, events.

`<hr />`

Usage	Horizontal rules are used to separate sections of a Web page.
Attributes	core, events.
	noshade="..." Displays the rule as a solid color.

`<i>...</i>`

Usage	Italicized text.
Attributes	core, i18n, events.

`<small>...</small>`

Usage	Small text.
Attributes	core, i18n, events.

`<tt>...</tt>`

Usage	Teletype (or monospaced) text.
Attributes	core, i18n, events.

Lists

You can organize text into a more structured outline by creating lists. Lists can be nested.

`<dd>...</dd>`

Usage	The definition description used in a `<dl>` (definition list) element.
Attributes	core, i18n, events.
Notes	Can contain block-level content, such as the `<p>` element.

`<dl>...</dl>`

Usage	Creates a definition list.
Attributes	core, i18n, events.
	compact="compact" Deprecated. Compacts the displayed list.
Notes	Must contain at least one `<dt>` or `<dd>` element in any order.

`<dt>...</dt>`

Usage	The definition term (or label) used within a `<dl>` (definition list) element.
Attributes	core, i18n, events.
Notes	Must contain text (which can be modified by text markup elements).

`<li>...</li>`

Usage	Defines a list item within a list.
Attributes	`core`, `i18n`, `events`.
	`type="..."` Changes the numbering style (`1`, `a`, `A`, `i`, `I`) in ordered lists, or the bullet style (`disc`, `square`, `circle`) in unordered lists.
	`value="..."` Sets the numbering to the given integer beginning with the current list item.

`<ol>...</ol>`

Usage	Creates an ordered list.
Attributes	`core`, `i18n`, `events`.
	`start="..."` Sets the starting number to the chosen integer.
Notes	Must contain at least one list item.

`<ul>...</ul>`

Usage	Creates an unordered list.
Attributes	`core`, `i18n`, `events`.
Notes	Must contain at least one list item.

Links

Hyperlinking is fundamental to HTML. These elements enable you to link to other documents, other locations within a document, or external files.

`<a>...</a>`

Usage	Used to define links and anchors.
Attributes	`core, i18n, events`.

`charset="..."` Character encoding of the resource.

`name="..."` Defines an anchor.

`href="..."` The URL of the linked resource.

`target="..."` Determines where the resource is displayed (user-defined name, `_blank, _parent, _self, _top`).

`rel="..."` Forward link types.

`rev="..."` Reverse link types.

`accesskey="..."` Assigns a hotkey to this element.

`shape="..."` Enables you to define client-side imagemaps using defined shapes (`default, rect, circle, poly`).

`coords="..."` Sets the size of the shape using pixel or percentage lengths.

`tabindex="..."` Sets the tabbing order between elements with a defined `tabindex`.

Tables

Tables are meant to display data in a tabular format. Tables are also widely used for page layout purposes.

\<caption>...\</caption>

Usage	Displays a table caption.
Attributes	core, i18n, events.

\<table>...\</table>

Usage	Creates a table.
Attributes	core, i18n, events.

width="..." Table width.

cols="..." The number of columns.

border="..." The width in pixels of a border around the table.

frame="..." Sets the visible sides of a table (void, above, below, hsides, lhs, rhs, vsides, box, border).

rules="..." Sets the visible rules within a table (none, groups, rows, cols, all).

cellspacing="..." Spacing between cells.

cellpadding="..." Spacing in cells.

\<td>...\</td>

Usage	Defines a cell's contents.
Attributes	core, i18n, events.

axis="..." Abbreviated name.

axes="..." axis names listing row and column headers pertaining to the cell.

rowspan="..." The number of rows spanned by a cell.

colspan="..." The number of columns spanned by a cell.

char="..." Sets a character on which the column aligns.

charoff="..." Offset to the first alignment character on a line.

<th>...</th>

Usage

Defines the cell contents of the table header.

Attributes

core, i18n, events.

axis="..." Abbreviated name.

axes="..." axis names listing row and column headers pertaining to the cell.

rowspan="..." The number of rows spanned by a cell.

colspan="..." The number of columns spanned by a cell.

char="..." Sets a character on which the column aligns.

charoff="..." Offset to the first alignment character on a line.

<tr>...</tr>

Usage

Defines a row of table cells.

Attributes

core, i18n, events.

char="..."   Sets a character on which
the column aligns.

charoff="..."   Offset to the first alignment character on a line.

Frames

Frames create new panels in the Web browser window that are used to
display content from different source documents.

<frame />

Usage   Defines a frame.

Attributes   name="..."   The name of a frame.

src="..."   The source to be displayed in
a frame.

frameborder="..."   Toggles the border
between frames (0, 1).

marginwidth="..."   Sets the space
between the frame border and content.

marginheight="..."   Sets the space
between the frame border and content.

noresize   Disables sizing.

scrolling="..."   Determines scrollbar
presence (auto, yes, no).

Notes   Use the Frameset DTD.

`<frameset>...</frameset>`

Usage	Defines the layout of frames within a window.
Attributes	`rows="..."` The number of rows.
	`cols="..."` The number of columns.
	`onload="..."` The intrinsic event triggered when the document loads.
	`onunload="..."` The intrinsic event triggered when the document unloads.
Notes	Use the Frameset DTD.

`<iframe>...</iframe>`

Usage	Creates an inline frame.
Attributes	`name="..."` The name of the frame.
	`src="..."` The source to be displayed in a frame.
	`frameborder="..."` Toggles the border between frames (0, 1).
	`marginwidth="..."` Sets the space between the frame border and content.
	`marginheight="..."` Sets the space between the frame border and content.
	`scrolling="..."` Determines scrollbar presence (auto, yes, no).
	`height="..."` Height.
	`width="..."` Width.

`<noframes>`...`</noframes>`

Usage	Alternative content when frames are not supported.
Attributes	None.
Notes	Use the Frameset DTD. The `<body>` element must be included inside the `<noframes>` tag.

Embedded Content

Also called inclusions, embedded content applies to Java applets, imagemaps, and other multimedia or programmed content that is placed in a Web page to provide additional functionality.

Comments `<! -` ... `- >`

Usage	Used to insert notes or scripts that are not displayed by the browser.
Attributes	None.
Notes	Comments are not restricted to one line and can be any length. The end tag is not required to be on the same line as the start tag.

`<img />`

Usage	Includes an image in the document.
Attributes	`core`, `i18n`, `events`.
	`src="..."` The URL of the image.
	`alt="..."` Alternative text to display.
	`height="..."` The height of the image.

`width="..."`   The width of the image.

`border="..."`   Border width.

`hspace="..."`   The horizontal space separating the image from other content.

`vspace="..."`   The vertical space separating the image from other content.

`usemap="..."`   The URL to a client-side imagemap.

`ismap="ismap"`   Identifies a server-side imagemap.

`<map>...</map>`

Usage   When used with the `<area>` element, it creates a client-side imagemap.

Attributes   `core`.

`name="..."`   The name of the imagemap to be created.

`<object>...</object>`

Usage   Includes an object or applet.

Attributes   `core, i18n, events`.

`declare="declare"`   A flag that declares, but doesn't create an object.

`classid="..."`   The URL of the object's location.

`codebase="..."`   The URL for resolving URLs specified by other attributes.

`data="..."`   The URL to the object's data.

`type="..."`   The Internet content type for data.

`codetype="..."`   The Internet content type for the code.

`standby="..."`   Shows message while loading.

`height="..."`   The height of the object.

`width="..."`   The width of the object.

`border="..."`   Displays the border around an object.

`hspace="..."`   The space between the sides of the object and other page content.

`vspace="..."`   The space between the top and bottom of the object and other page content.

`usemap="..."`   The URL to an imagemap.

`shapes=`   Enables you to define areas to search for hyperlinks if the object is an image.

`name="..."`   The URL to submit as part of a form.

`tabindex="..."`   Sets the tabbing order between elements with a defined `tabindex`.

Style

Style sheets (both embedded and linked) are incorporated into an HTML document through the use of the `<style>` element.

`<style>...</style>`

Usage	Creates an internal style sheet.
Attributes	i18n.
	`type="..."` The Internet content type.
	`media="..."` Defines the destination medium (screen, print, projection, braille, speech, all).
	`title="..."` The title of the style.
Notes	Located within the `<head>` element.

Forms

Forms create an interface for the user to select options and return data to the Web server.

`<button>...</button>`

Usage	Creates a button.
Attributes	core, i18n, events.
	`name="..."` The button name.
	`value="..."` The value of the button.
	`type="..."` The button type (button, submit, reset).
	`disabled="..."` Sets the button state to disabled.

`tabindex="..."`   Sets the tabbing order between elements with a defined `tabindex`.

`onfocus="..."`   The event that occurs when the element receives focus.

`onblur="..."`   The event that occurs when the element loses focus.

`<form>...</form>`

Usage   Creates a form that holds controls for user input.

Attributes   `core`, `i18n`, `events`.

`action="..."`   The URL for the server action.

`method="..."`   The HTTP method (`get`, `post`). `get` is deprecated.

`enctype="..."`   Specifies the MIME (Internet media type).

`onsubmit="..."`   The intrinsic event that occurs when the form is submitted.

`onreset="..."`   The intrinsic event that occurs when the form is reset.

`target="..."`   Determines where the resource is displayed (user-defined name, `_blank`, `_parent`, `_self`, `_top`).

`accept-charset="..."`   The list of character encodings.

`<input />`

Usage	Defines controls used in forms.
Attributes	`core, i18n, events`.

`type="..."`   The type of input control (`text, password, checkbox, radio, submit, reset, file, hidden, image, button`).

`name="..."`   The name of the control (required except for `submit` and `reset`).

`value="..."`   The initial value of the control (required for radio and check-boxes).

`checked="checked"`   Sets the radio buttons to a checked state.

`disabled="..."`   Disables the control.

`readonly="..."`   For text password types.

`size="..."`   The width of the control in pixels except for text and password controls, which are specified in number of characters.

`maxlength="..."`   The maximum number of characters that can be entered.

`src="..."`   The URL to an image control type.

`alt="..."`   An alternative text description.

`usemap="..."`   The URL to a client-side imagemap.

`tabindex="..."`   Sets the tabbing order between elements with a defined `tabindex`.

`onfocus="..."`   The event that occurs when the element receives focus.

`onblur="..."`   The event that occurs when the element loses focus.

`onselect="..."`   Intrinsic event that occurs when the control is selected.

`onchange="..."`   Intrinsic event that occurs when the control is changed.

`accept="..."`   File types allowed for upload.

`<label>...</label>`

Usage   Labels a control.

Attributes   `core`, `i18n`, `events`.

`for="..."`   Associates a label with an identified control.

`disabled="..."`   Disables a control.

`accesskey="..."`   Assigns a hotkey to this element.

`onfocus="..."`   The event that occurs when the element receives focus.

`onblur="..."`   The event that occurs when the element loses focus.

`<legend>...</legend>`

Usage   Assigns a caption to a `fieldset`.

Attributes   `core`, `i18n`, `events`.

`accesskey="..."`   Assigns a hotkey to this element.

`<option>...</option>`

Usage	Specifies choices in a `<select>` element.
Attributes	`core, i18n, events`.

`selected="selected"`   Specifies whether the option is selected.

`disabled="disabled"`   Disables the control.

`value="..."`   The value submitted if a control is submitted.

`<select>...</select>`

Usage	Creates choices for the user to select.
Attributes	`core, i18n, events`.

`name="..."`   The name of the element.

`size="..."`   The height in number of visible rows.

`multiple="multiple"`   Allows multiple selections.

`disabled="disabled"`   Disables the control.

`tabindex="..."`   Sets the tabbing order between elements with a defined `tabindex`.

`onfocus="..."`   The event that occurs when the element receives focus.

`onblur="..."`   The event that occurs when the element loses focus.

`onselect="..."` Intrinsic event that occurs when the control is selected.

`onchange="..."` Intrinsic event that occurs when the control is changed.

`<textarea>...</textarea>`

Usage

Creates an area for user input with multiple lines.

Attributes

`core, i18n, events`.

`name="..."` The name of the control.

`rows="..."` The height in number of rows.

`cols="..."` The width in number of columns.

`disabled="disabled"` Disables the control.

`readonly="readonly"` Sets the displayed text to read-only status.

`tabindex="..."` Sets the tabbing order between elements with a defined `tabindex`.

`onfocus="..."` The event that occurs when the element receives focus.

`onblur="..."` The event that occurs when the element loses focus.

`onselect="..."` Intrinsic event that occurs when the control is selected.

onchange="..." Intrinsic event that
occurs when the control is changed.

Notes   Text to be displayed is placed within the
                     start and end tags.

Scripts

Scripting language is made available to process data and performs other
dynamic events through the <script> element.

<script>...</script>

Usage   The <script> element contains client-side
                     scripts that are executed by the browser.

Attributes   type="..." Script language Internet
                     content type.

                     src="..." The URL for the external
                     script.

Notes   You can set the default scripting language
                     in the <meta /> element.

<noscript>...</noscript>

Usage   Provides alternative content for browsers
                     unable to execute a script.

Attributes   None.

Common Attributes and Events

Four attributes are abbreviated as core in the preceding sections. They are

* id="..." A global identifier.

* class="..." A list of classes separated by spaces.

- `style="..."`   Style information.
- `title="..."`   Provides more information for a specific element, as opposed to the `<title>` element, which entitles the entire Web page.

Two attributes for internationalization (`i18n`) are abbreviated as `i18n`:

- `lang="..."`   The language identifier.
- `dir=c`   The text direction (`ltr`, `rtl`).

The following intrinsic events are abbreviated `events`:

- `OnClick="..."`   A pointing device (such as a mouse) was single-clicked.
- `OnDblClick="..."`   A pointing device (such as a mouse) was double-clicked.
- `OnMouseDown="..."`   A mouse button was clicked and held down.
- `OnMouseUp="..."`   A mouse button that was clicked and held down was released.
- `OnMouseOver="..."`   A mouse moved the cursor over an object.
- `OnMouseMove="..."`   The mouse was moved.
- `OnMouseOut="..."`   A mouse moved the cursor off an object.
- `OnKeyPress="..."`   A key was pressed and released.
- `OnKeyDown="..."`   A key was pressed and held down.
- `OnKeyUp="..."`   A key that was pressed has been released.

APPENDIX B

Style Sheet Quick Reference

Cascading Style Sheets enable Web authors to attach style (for example, fonts, spacing, and colors) to HTML documents. By separating the presentation style of documents from the content of documents, the style sheet specification simplifies Web authoring and site maintenance. This appendix provides a quick reference to some of the most common style sheet properties.

 Tip This appendix is based on the information provided in the *CSS 2.0 Specification W3C Recommendation* (revised on May 12, 1998). The latest version of this standard can be found at http://www. w3.org/TR/REC-CSS2/.

To make the information readily accessible, this appendix organizes style sheet properties by their function in the following order:

- Background

- Border

- Text

- Lists

- Page

- Tables

- Positioning

The elements are listed alphabetically within each section, and the following information is presented:

- Usage   A general description of the property.

- Values   Lists the values of the property with a short description of their effect.

- Initial Value   Lists the default value of the property. It is not necessary to set this value.

- Notes   Relates any special considerations when using the property.

Background

This sets the style for the background of a page, table, or other element.

background-color

Usage	Sets the background color of an element.
Values	`<color>` The hex number (or text equivalent) of the preferred color.
	`transparent` The same background as the underlying element.
	`inherit` The same background as the parent element.
Initial Value	`transparent`

background-image

Usage	Sets the background image for an element.
Values	url("...") The URL for the background image.
	inherit The same background as the parent element.
	none No image.
Initial Value	none

Border

Sets the border styles for the page, text, table, and image elements.

border-color

Usage	Sets the border color for an element.
Values	<color> The hex number (or text equivalent) of the preferred color.
	inherit The same background as the parent element.
	none No image.
Initial Value	transparent
Notes	Set the color for specific borders using the border-top-color, border-right-color, border-bottom-color, and border-left-color properties.

border-style

Usage	Sets the style of the border for an element.
Values	dotted A series of small dots form the border.

`dashed`   A series of dashes form the border.

`solid`   A narrow, solid line forms the border.

`double`   Double, narrow, solid lines form the border.

`groove`   A narrow carved line forms the border.

`ridge`   A narrow raised line forms the border.

`inset`   The border makes the entire element appear to be embedded.

`outset`   The border makes the entire element appear to be raised.

`inherit`   The same border as the parent element.

`none`   No border.

Initial Value   `none`

Notes   Set the position of the border with the `border-top-style`, `border-right-style`, `border-bottom-style`, and `border-left-style` properties.

border-width

Usage   Sets the width of the border for an element.

Values   `thin`   A thin line forms the border.

`medium`   A medium line forms the border.

`thick`   A thick line forms the border.

`inherit`   The same border position as the parent element.

Initial Value	`medium`
Notes	Set the width of specific borders using the `border-top-width`, `border-right-width`, `border-bottom-width`, and `border-left-width` properties.

Text

Sets the fonts, colors, positioning, and other styles for the text elements.

text-align

Usage	Sets the alignment of the text element.
Values	`left` The text is aligned on the left side.
	`right` The text is aligned on the right side.
	`center` The text is aligned from the center.
	`justify` The text is aligned on both the left and right sides.
	`inherit` The same border position as the parent element.
Initial Value	Depends on the browser settings.

text-decoration

Usage	Sets the format of the text element.
Values	`underline` A line appears under the text.
	`overline` A line appears over the text.
	`line-through` A line appears horizontally through the center of the text.

blink   The text blinks.

inherit   The same border position as the parent element.

Initial Value   none (or underline for links).

text-indent

Usage   Sets the spacing before the text element relative to the surrounding elements.

Values   <length>   The indent spacing is a fixed length.

<percentage>   The indent spacing is a percentage of the containing element.

inherit   The same spacing as the parent element.

Initial Value   0

color

Usage   Sets the color of the font.

Values   <color>   The hex number (or text equivalent) of the preferred color.

inherit   The same color as the parent element.

Initial Value   Depends on the browser setting.

font-family

Usage   Sets the font to be used.

Values   <family name>   The name of the font family as it appears in your editor.

`<generic family>` Sets a generic font set dependent on the user's computer (`serif`, `sans-serif`, `fantasy`, and `monospace`).

`inherit` The same family as the parent element.

Initial Value   Depends on the browser setting.

font-size

Usage   Sets the font size.

Values   `<size>` The size of the font. Can be relative to the parent element as a percentage, or can be a fixed size.

`inherit` The same size as the parent element.

Initial Value   `medium`

font-style

Usage   Sets the style of the font.

Values   `normal` No special format to the font.

`italic` The font appears in italics.

`inherit` The same style as the parent element.

Initial Value   `normal`

font-weight

Usage   Sets the weight of the font.

Values   `<weight>` The weight of the font as `normal`, `bold`, `bolder`, or `lighter`.

100–900   The weight of the font as a percentage of the parent font.

inherit   The same weight as the parent element.

Initial Value   normal

 Tip   Links can use all the same properties as other text elements, but you need to remember the link types.

- a:link

- a:visited

- a:active

- a:hover (IE only)

List

Sets the style for lists.

list-style-image

Usage   Sets an image to replace the list bullets.

Values   url("...")   The URL for the image.

none   No images.

inherit   The same image as the parent element.

Initial Value   none

list-style-type

Usage   Sets the style of the list bullets.

Values   <shape>   The bullets can be set to disc
                 (closed circle), circle (open circle), or
                 square (closed square).

                 <alignment>   The bullets can be aligned
                 around decimal or decimal-leading-zero.

                 <text>   The bullets can be replaced with
                 roman numerals (lower-roman, upper-roman),
                 latin numerals (lower-latin, upper-latin),
                 or American alphabet characters (lower-
                 alpha, upper-alpha).

                 inherit   The same bullet type as the parent
                 element.

Initial Value   disc

Page Properties

Style affects the entire page.

margin

Usage   Sets the margins for the page.

Values   <margin-width>   The width of the margin in
                 percentage or in fixed width.

                 inherit   The same spacing as the parent
                 element.

Initial Value   0

Notes   Set specific margins using the margin-top,
                 margin-right, margin-bottom, and margin-
                 left properties.

Table Properties

Sets the style for the table elements.

caption-side

Usage	Sets the position of the caption relative to the element.
Values	`top` The caption appears at the top of the element.
	`bottom` The caption appears at the bottom of the element.
	`left` The caption appears to the left of the element.
	`right` The caption appears to the right of the element.
	`inherit` The same position as the parent element.
Initial Value	0

empty-cells

Usage	Specifies the treatment of empty table cells.
Values	`show` Empty cells are treated the same as nonempty cells.
	`hide` Empty cells are not displayed.
	`inherit` The same spacing as the parent element.
Initial Value	`show`

padding

Usage	Sets the space that surrounds the element.
Values	`<length>` Sets the table padding to a fixed length.
	`<percentage>` Sets the table padding to a percentage.
Initial Value	0
Notes	Set specific padding using the `padding-top`, `padding-right`, `padding-bottom`, and `padding-left` properties.

float

Usage	Sets the spacing before the text element relative to the surrounding elements.
Values	`left` The content of the element floats to the left.
	`right` The content of the element floats to the right.
	`none` The content does not float.
Initial Value	none

Positioning

Sets the position of all elements.

vertical-align

Usage	Sets the vertical alignment of the element relative to the surrounding elements.
Values	`baseline` The element aligns with the baseline of surrounding elements.

sub or super   The element is subscripted or superscripted respectively.

top, middle, bottom   The element is aligned with the top, middle, or bottom of surrounding elements respectively.

text-top, text-bottom   The element is aligned with the top or bottom of surrounding text elements.

<length>   The alignment as a fixed length.

<percentage>   The alignment as a percentage.

inherit   The same alignment as the parent element.

Initial Value   baseline

height

Usage   Sets the height of the element.

Values   <length>   The height as a fixed length.

<percentage>   The height as a percentage of the containing element.

auto   The height depends on the value of other properties.

inherit   The same spacing as the parent element.

Initial Value   auto

width

Usage	Sets the width of the element.
Values	`<length>` The width as a fixed length.
	`<percentage>` The width as a percentage of the containing element.
	`auto` The width depends on the value of other properties.
	`inherit` The same spacing as the parent element.
Initial Value	`auto`

INDEX

X - Y - Z

Other Related Titles

Sams Teach Yourself Web Publishing with HTML and XHTML in 21 Days, Professional Reference Edition, Third Edition
Laura Lemay
ISBN: 0-672-32-2048
$49.99 US/$74.95 CAN

Sams Teach Yourself ASP.NET in 24 Hours, Second Edition
Joseph Martin, Brett Tomson
ISBN: 0-672-32126-2
$39.99 US/$59.95 CAN

Sams Teach Yourself XML in 21 Days, Second Edition
Devan Shepherd
ISBN: 0-672-32093-2
$39.99 US/$59.95 CAN

Sams Teach Yourself Macromedia Flash 5 in 24 Hours
Phillip Kerman
ISBN: 0-672-31892-X
$24.99 US/$37.95 CAN

PHP and MySQL Web Development
Luke Welling and Laura Thomson
ISBN: 0-672-31784-2
$49.99 US/$74.95 CAN

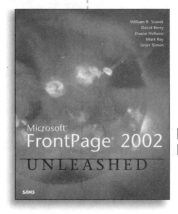

FrontPage 2002 Unleashed
William Stanek, et al
ISBN: 0-672-32205-6
$49.99 US/$74.95 CAN

Sams Teach Yourself JavaScript in 24 Hours, Second Edition
Michael Moncur
ISBN: 0-672-32025-8
$24.99 US/$37.95 CAN

SAMS
www.samspublishing.com